Lothar-Rüdiger Lütge

Yuval Noah Harari:
What He Says. What He Thinks.
And What That Has to Do With
God.

Publisher:
BoD · Books on Demand GmbH,
Überseering 33, 22297 Hamburg,
bod@bod.de
Printed by:
Libri Plureos GmbH,
Friedensallee 273, 22763 Hamburg

ISBN: 978-3-8192-3061-5

Western civilization has survived the invasion of Genghis Khan from the East, the Ottoman Empire from the South, and two world wars originating from within. But whether it will survive its own intellectuals is much more doubtful.

(Thomas Sowell, American economist, and historian)

Lothar-Rüdiger Lütge

Yuval Noah Harari:
What He Says. What He Thinks.
And What That Has to Do With
God.

Table of Contents

Introduction: Why This Book Is Necessary

Who is Yuval Noah Harari?

Yuval Noah Harari is an Israeli historian and philosopher, born in 1976 in Kiryat Ata near Haifa. He teaches at the Hebrew University of Jerusalem, where he initially specialized in medieval military history before gradually shifting his focus to macro-history, the history of science, and ultimately to the future of humanity. Harari earned his doctorate at Oxford and is today considered one of the most influential intellectuals of the 21st century. His work operates at the intersection of historical scholarship, anthropology, future studies, and the ethics of technology.

Harari gained international recognition through his popular science bestsellers, which are among his most influential and widely distributed works:

Sapiens: A Brief History of Humankind (2011)

Homo Deus: A Brief History of Tomorrow (2015)

21 Lessons for the 21st Century (2018)

Nexus: A Brief History of Information Networks from the Stone Age to Artificial Intelligence (2024)

These books have been translated into over 65 languages and have sold more than 40 million copies. They are published by major international publishing houses and are regularly featured in public debates, readings, and interviews.

At international conferences, Harari is received like a rock star of the global intellectual scene. His ideas and assessments are taken seriously both in political and technological circles – which makes him a figure of considerable societal relevance.

But who is Harari – beyond the media image?

Harari identifies as a secular humanist. He analyzes religions as historical myths but does not consider them metaphysically true. His thinking is deeply shaped by Darwinism, evolutionary psychology, and neurobiological models of human behavior. He does not merely aim to interpret the past but also seeks to shape – or at least frame – the future. In this sense, he stands as a representative of a new generation of secular intellectuals who, with scientific authority, articulate foundational anthropological and philosophical claims.

And this is precisely where Harari becomes the subject of our engagement. His books do not merely offer theses about the past and future of humanity – they also propose a very specific image of the human being. This image is radically materialistic, deterministic, technocratic – and, ultimately, nihilistic. It portrays the human not as a metaphysical being, but as a biological algorithm, whose individual subjectivity and freedom are, in the final analysis, illusions.

This worldview is not merely Harari's personal opinion – it is gaining influence. And it has consequences: for how the human being is understood in education and science, for the ethical foundations of technology and medicine, and for the visions of society shaped by elites.

That is why we are writing this book.

His Major Works and Their Global Reach

Yuval Noah Harari has authored several works that have attracted significant international attention. At the heart of his publications lies a recurring question: What is the nature of the human being? However, he does not approach this question from a metaphysical angle, but rather from historical, biological, and increasingly technocratic perspectives. His books have been translated into more than 65 languages and have sold over 40 million copies. This places Harari among the most widely read and influential intellectuals of our time.

What follows is an overview of his most important and impactful works:

Sapiens: A Brief History of Humankind (2011)
This book marked Harari's breakthrough and became a worldwide bestseller. It narrates the story of Homo sapiens from the Stone Age to the present – not as a classical chronology, but as a sweeping synthesis of intellectual and anthropological history. Harari

identifies three major "revolutions" that shaped humankind:

The Cognitive Revolution (around 70,000 years ago), when humans began thinking in complex stories and myths;

The Agricultural Revolution, which led to settled life and the emergence of complex societies;

The Scientific Revolution, beginning in the 16th century and culminating in modernity.

Harari argues that the human self-image – including religion, morality, and freedom – consists of cultural constructs that serve social organization rather than reflecting any objective truth. Humanity, in this view, does not appear as the "crown of creation" but rather as an accidental winner in the evolutionary game of dominance.

Homo Deus: A Brief History of Tomorrow (2015)
In Homo Deus, Harari ventures a forecast of humanity's future. He begins with the claim

that humankind – at least in affluent regions – has largely "conquered" major historical problems such as famine, war, and plague. Now, he suggests, we are turning to new goals: immortality, happiness, divinity.

A central theme is Harari's vision of "Dataism": a new worldview in which information and its processing become the highest value. Human beings are seen essentially as biological algorithms, whose thinking and decisions are entirely explainable and, eventually, controllable. In this framework, the boundaries between human and machine blur, and the biological body loses significance. Artificial intelligence and biotechnology represent, for Harari, the next stage in evolution – potentially even a replacement for Homo sapiens.

According to Harari, humans may learn to "play God" – not in a religious sense, but as technological entities. The book offers no hope for metaphysical meaning or divine presence; on the contrary, Harari envisions a world in which meaning, soul, and freedom increasingly appear as myths.

21 Lessons for the 21st Century (2018)
This work is less a continuous argument and more a collection of essays addressing current questions: What does truth mean in the age of fake news? How do we deal with terrorism, migration, artificial intelligence, and climate change? What roles do education, religion, and the nation-state still play in the 21st century?

Harari presents a wide array of challenges facing modern humans – as political, technological, and emotional beings. His general posture remains skeptical of traditional solutions: he sees no lasting stability in religion, nationalism, or even liberal ideals. Instead, he calls for a "new enlightenment" based on scientific insight, global cooperation, and technological adaptation.

Despite some useful reflections, the book – like its predecessors – is underpinned by a worldview that relativizes or outright denies meaning, transcendence, and subjective freedom.

Nexus: A Brief History of Information Networks – from the Stone Age to Artificial Intelligence (2024)

In his most recent work to date, Harari explores the development of information systems as the driving force of human history. From his perspective, it is not divine revelations or philosophical ideas that shape societies, but rather networks of communication and data processing – from the first spoken word to the invention of writing, and onward to big data and AI.

Nexus is divided into three main sections:

Human Networks – the earliest forms of information dissemination: language, myth, religion, administration;

The Inorganic Network – the rise of machines, algorithms, and global data flows;

Computer Politics – the political dimension of modern information power, the risks of algorithmic world governance, and the urgent need for regulatory oversight.

Here too, Harari remains true to his vision: there is no metaphysical meaning, only functional structures. Once again, the human being is not creator or image of God, but a node in a vast stream of data.

Conclusion

Harari's works have reached millions – not despite, but perhaps because of their cultural pessimism and technocratic tone. His ability to present complex ideas in accessible language has earned him the status of a "public intellectual." But such popularity does not come without consequences:

Anyone who reduces human freedom, identity, and dignity to functional illusions is not merely describing the world –
he is shaping it.

Why His Ideas Matter

The significance of Yuval Noah Harari lies not only in the popularity of his books, but in the fact that his ideas are playing an increasingly prominent role in public thought. What he writes is not merely read –

it influences.
And it does so on multiple levels.

1. A Global Public Intellectual

Harari is not a theorist confined to the academic ivory tower; he is a public figure who regularly speaks at international conferences. His theses are taken up by leading politicians and technology entrepreneurs. Among his declared readers are heads of state, CEOs, and the founders and board members of major global tech companies.

Through interviews, essays, and keynote speeches, Harari consistently shapes the discourse around major questions of the future – from artificial intelligence and digital control to biotechnology, freedom, education, and governance. Many of his statements find their way into political and technological frameworks – not as binding programs, but as ideological reference points within which thinking unfolds.

2. The Appeal of Clarity

Harari writes in an accessible, often elegant language. He offers orientation in complexity and gives readers the feeling that they are gaining a coherent view of the forces shaping our world. This ability to "make sense of the world" makes him attractive to many – especially in an age marked by information overload, uncertainty, and technological upheaval.

But this is precisely what gives his theses their power:
They sound plausible, appear scientifically grounded, and align with a widely accepted secular worldview.
These are not fringe opinions – they are convictions that many people, consciously or unconsciously, already hold within themselves.

3. A Worldview in Transition

Harari does not merely describe the present – he interprets it.
And in his interpretation, the human being loses his role as a free, unique, spiritual being.
The self becomes a biological algorithm, freedom a neurological illusion, and meaning a cultural construction.
His worldview is internally consistent – but it transforms the way we see ourselves:

from subject to system,
from image of God to information processor.

This perspective is already influencing debates in education, science, politics, and ethics. It is supplying the conceptual foundations for developments long underway – in surveillance technology, genetic research, education policy, and the self-understanding of state and economy.

That is precisely why a serious engagement with Harari's thinking is necessary.

Not because we wish to criticize a person –
but because we must understand the anthropology that is gaining ground here,
and what is at stake if this worldview pre-
vails.

Our goal is to help readers understand what
Harari is actually saying –
and what that means for us as human beings.

We are not questioning an author –
we are questioning an idea:

the idea that the human being is empty,
without essence,
without direction,
without God.

Influence on Politics, Tech Elites, and Public Discourse

Yuval Noah Harari is not only the author of bestselling books, but also a sought-after conversation partner for leading figures in politics, business, and technology. His presence in public debate extends far beyond traditional science communication – he has become a thought leader in global discussions about the future of humanity.

1. Political Resonance

Harari has been received, cited, and engaged by heads of state, government leaders, and influential think tanks. Some of his most prominent interlocutors include:

Barack Obama, who publicly praised Harari's works and insights;

Angela Merkel, who discussed Harari's perspectives on digitization in a televised conversation;

Emmanuel Macron, with whom Harari spoke about European values and technological development;

Olaf Scholz, who, as Germany's finance minister, shared a stage with Harari to discuss the transformation of the labor market.

Harari's reflections on artificial intelligence, governance, global cooperation, and "posthumanism" are finding their way into political narratives – particularly in discussions around platform regulation, education models, and the design of digital infrastructures. His voice often functions like an intellectual litmus test:

Anyone addressing the future of humanity seemingly cannot bypass Harari.

2. Tech Corporations as Echo Chambers

Harari's influence is especially pronounced in the technology sector – among companies whose business models revolve around data processing, automation, and biotechnology.

Mark Zuckerberg (Meta/Facebook) engaged Harari in a public conversation on social networks, surveillance, and freedom of expression.

Bill Gates expressed admiration for Harari's books and highlighted their relevance for the future of education on his personal blog.

Elon Musk, though not always in agreement, has referenced Harari's theses on multiple occasions – particularly regarding artificial intelligence.

In these circles, Harari is not seen as a critic of the tech world, but rather as a provocative catalyst:
He articulates the big questions that technological progress raises – often without taking a clear position, but with considerable rhetorical power.

3. Media Presence and Cultural Reach

Harari appears regularly in major international media outlets – including The New York Times, The Guardian, Die Zeit, Le

Monde, CNN, and the BBC. His books are found in school libraries, universities, and professional development institutions around the world. In German-speaking countries, Harari is firmly embedded in both the educated middle class and cultural-political discourse.

Through essays, podcasts, video interviews, and TED Talks, his ideas are disseminated in easily accessible formats. In this way, he shapes not only decision-makers but also a broader public seeking orientation in a world that appears increasingly technologized, fragmented, and complex.

Conclusion

Harari is not "just a historian" –

he is an architect of cultural narratives.
His ideas circulate in the very spaces where decisions about the future are made.
They influence mindsets, language, and priorities – not by issuing directives, but by offering compelling frames of interpretation.

And that is precisely why it is necessary to examine these narratives more closely –
in order to understand them,
and, where appropriate,
to question them.

The Quiet Cult Status of a Technocrat

In recent years, Yuval Noah Harari has assumed a special role in Western public discourse:
He has become a mirror for the questions the modern world asks about itself.
What sets him apart from other intellectuals is not only the breadth of his topics, but the manner in which he presents them: calm, objective, unpretentious –
yet delivered with a near-prophetic confidence when it comes to the future of humanity.

In many circles of debate, Harari appears as a kind of modern seer, sketching the contours of what lies ahead based on data, history, and technological trends. His voice often combines sober analysis with a distinct interpretive authority – a rare combination that has earned him an almost cult-like status.

This status does not manifest in fanatic devotion, but rather in subtle authority:
Harari's statements are rarely questioned.

They are quoted, shared, and discussed – but often without a systematic examination of their premises.

Precisely because he presents himself so rationally, his claims seem "reasonable."

And that is exactly why they require critical scrutiny.

In many circles – political, academic, educational – Harari is seen as a "voice of the future."

His influence does not rest on institutional power but on semantic primacy:

He names developments before others know how to interpret them –

and in doing so, he provides the very language through which we come to think about them.

But what if the language we use to think – already limits our thinking?

This is precisely the point where our engagement with Harari's work begins. Not to "debunk" him, but to examine whether the image of the human being he presents truly does justice to what the human being is.

Why a Critical Response Is Needed

The ideas of Yuval Noah Harari are well-formulated, rhetorically powerful, and widely disseminated.
They offer orientation in a complex world – seemingly neutral, scientific, enlightened.
Yet beneath the surface, they reveal a vision of the human being that answers fundamental philosophical and existential questions in a direction that deserves to be examined.

For if one follows Harari's thinking to its logical conclusion, a striking picture emerges:
A human being with no self, no freedom, and no need for meaning.
In his worldview, the person appears as a biologically determined, data-processing entity – embedded in systems larger than itself, but ultimately devoid of purpose or moral structure.

Everything that humans perceive as meaningful – love, conscience, hope, religion, vocation – is, for Harari, reduced to functionality or evolutionary advantage.
Meaning is a side effect.

Will is an illusion.
The subject is a myth.

But if that were true —
to whom is Harari speaking?

What does it mean to write books, give lectures, or propose visions of the future
if there are no free readers,
no acting subjects,
no morally accountable recipients?

This is not a rhetorical question.
It is a fundamental one.
And it reveals something crucial:
Harari's worldview is not merely a new interpretation of reality —

it is an attempt to redefine the human being from the inside out.
Quietly, gradually, dressed in scientific vocabulary.
But what is at stake is nothing less than our understanding of what it means to be human
—

and whether there is still such a thing as the human being at all.

That is why a critical response is necessary.

Not out of polemic.
Not out of ideological opposition.
But out of a simple and profound need:

the need to preserve the human being –
as an individual,
as a spiritual being,
as a free self in relation to a transcendent reality.

This book seeks to make a contribution toward reclaiming a view of the human person that is grounded not in algorithms, but in experience;
not in utility, but in truth;
not in statistics, but in meaning.

It seeks to offer, against the image of the functional human,
a vision of the real human.
Not by repeating old beliefs –
but by showing that belief itself
is what makes us
capable of being human.

Part I: The Hollowed-Out Human – An Analysis of Harari's Worldview

Prologue to Part I: Taking Harari at His Word

The following chapters form the first part of our book: a deeper engagement with some of Yuval Noah Harari's central claims. Our aim is not to provide a comprehensive overview of his entire body of work, but rather to illuminate his thinking through three striking statements –
statements that touch on the fundamental pillars of his worldview:

Identity, freedom, and meaning.

We have deliberately chosen only a few, but highly significant, quotations –
not to take them out of context,
but to expose the inner core of his philosophy.

Harari is not a cautious thinker.
He expresses himself clearly, pointedly, and with far-reaching implications.
This is the source of his influence –

and also the point where his thought be-comes vulnerable.

We do not intend to criticize his statements, but to analyze them:

What does Harari actually say?

What assumptions underlie his claims?

What logically follows if one carries these thoughts to their conclusion?

In doing so, we will strictly adhere to the standards of rational and intellectual integrity.
We will not make unfounded claims, but simply make visible what is already there.
We will refrain from polemic judgment and instead draw out what is already implicit in his words.

Because sometimes, no refutation is neces-sary.
It is enough to shine light on what has been said – and compare it to the human being who reads it.

Chapter 1 – The Dissolution of the Self

Key Quote:

"The single authentic self is as real as the eternal soul, Santa Claus and the Easter Bunny. If I look really deep within myself, the seeming unity that I take for granted dissolves into a cacophony of conflicting voices, none of which is 'my true self'. Humans aren't individuals. They are 'dividuals'."

(Yuval Noah Harari, Homo Deus: A History of Tomorrow)

This can be summarized as follows:

Human beings are not individuals. They are dividuals – fragmented entities composed of networks of biochemical and neurological processes, with no unified or enduring self.

Part 1: What Harari Says – and What He Means

We analyze the content of this statement and show how it dissolves the classical understanding of individuality.

Part 2: The Premises – Harari's Scientific Reductionism
We uncover the assumptions underlying his thinking: biologism, materialism, functionalism.

Part 3: The Consequences – If There Is No Indivisible Self
What follows for identity, conscience, responsibility, and human dignity?

Part 4: A First Contrast – The Experience of the Self as Starting Point
A preparatory step toward the counter-argument: the experience of "I am" as a fact, not a construct.

1. What Harari Says – and What He Means

Harari's thesis:

Human beings are not individuals. They are dividuals – divisible entities made up of a network of biochemical and neurological processes, without a unified or unchanging self.

With this claim, Harari touches one of the most sensitive and foundational concepts in the intellectual history of the Western world: the individual – the "indivisible," the "singular," the "unique."
Since antiquity – and even more so through the influence of the Christian understanding of the person – the individual has been regarded as the bearer of consciousness, responsibility, dignity, and freedom.
It is that which is absolutely irreplaceable and inimitable in every human being.

Harari challenges this concept – and not merely in nuances, but radically.
His thesis is clear: humans are not individuals. They are "dividuals."

49

The term was not coined by him, but he uses it with a specific purpose:
to convey the idea that the human being possesses no inner, stable core of being.
What we call the "self," for Harari, is not a unity, but a temporary arrangement of biochemical processes – comparable to a network of electrical impulses that constantly shifts and rearranges.

This means:

There is no enduring self – only reactions, processes, and configurations.
The human being, in this worldview, is not a being with an "interior," but the sum of externally measurable phenomena.
Thinking, feeling, remembering, deciding – all of this is not seen as expression of a self, but as the result of neural algorithms.

With this view, Harari aligns himself with a current of modern theories that seek to dissolve the subject – such as the neurobiological thesis of the "self as illusion" (promoted by thinkers like Thomas Metzinger, Daniel Dennett, or Patricia Churchland).

But Harari goes a step further:

He presents this view as the new normal.
The human being is no more than what science today can describe about him – and, in Harari's view, that is already enough to replace the old image of "I am."

It is important to grasp this point:
Harari does not merely deny the metaphysical depth of the human being –
he denies that there is any unified subject that persists through time at all.
For him, identity is a narrative trick of the brain – useful for communication, but without any ontological basis.
The human, one might paraphrase him, is a story the brain tells itself about itself.

What may sound like an academic abstraction has far-reaching implications.
For if there is no true self,

then there is no one who experiences.
There is no agent who thinks, feels, loves, or believes –
only reactions, patterns, and networks.

This is the beginning of the dissolution of the self.

2. The Premises – Harari's Scientific Reductionism

Harari's assertion that the human being is not an individual but a "dividual" is not the result of confusion or rhetorical misstep.
Rather, it follows directly from a particular way of thinking that has become dominant in large parts of modern science and philosophy:

naturalistic reductionism.

This approach is based on the assumption that all phenomena – including consciousness, self-awareness, will, and thought – can be fully explained in terms of physical, chemical, or biological processes.
In this view, there is nothing "within" the human being that cannot be accounted for by molecules, neurons, genes, or environmental stimuli.
What was once referred to as "spirit" or "soul" is now understood as a function of the brain – no longer a substance, but an effect.

Harari not only adopts this paradigm –

he carries it to its logical end.
His underlying assumptions can be summarized as follows:

The human being is a biological algorithm.
Thoughts, feelings, and memories are not expressions of an inner self but the output of computational processes in the brain – triggered by environmental factors, genetic disposition, and biochemical states.

There is no immutable instance within the human person.
Everything we experience as "I" – continuity, individuality, memory – is a construction, an illusion generated by the brain, which is trained to recognize patterns and impose order where none inherently exists.

What cannot be measured does not exist.
Harari's worldview is grounded in an empiricist ideal of knowledge: only that which can be quantified and scientifically observed counts as "real."
Everything else – subjective experience, spiritual intuition, metaphysical depth – is

dismissed as unreliable, irrelevant, or unsci-
entific.

This mode of thinking is not new.
It traces its roots back to Descartes' dualism,
but was significantly reinforced in the 19th
century by Darwinism and, later, by developments in neuroscience and computer science.

Harari brings all of these strands together
into a single, sharpened conclusion:

The human being is fully explainable – and
therefore, fully replaceable.

What defines us is not inner essence, but
outer function.
And this function, so the reasoning goes, can
one day be performed by machines – better,
more efficiently, and more reliably.

What unfolds in the background here is a
profound disenchantment of the human being.
For if there is no inner core, then man is no
longer a someone,

but merely a something – one system among many,
one object among objects.

It is precisely these premises that lead Harari to not merely question the classical awareness of self,
but to abolish it altogether.

And that raises the question:

What follows from this?

3. The Consequences – If There Is No Indivisible Self

If Harari is right – if the human being is not an individual but a decomposable, processual construct without a stable core of being –

then the consequences are far-reaching.
Not just for one's self-understanding, but for ethics, law, education, medicine, politics –
and ultimately, for every form of human community.

Because the image we have of the human being shapes how we treat one another –
as subjects or objects,
as bearers of dignity,
or as functional units within a system.

1. The Collapse of Identity

If the human being no longer has an inner center – no continuity of self, but only a sequence of neuronal states –
then personal identity begins to dissolve.
Who am I, if there is no "I"?

Who is responsible for my actions, if my will is merely a product of biochemistry?
Who is the one who remembers, chooses, suffers, or loves?

In Harari's model, none of this remains.
Identity becomes an illusion – a story the brain tells itself, useful perhaps, but not true.
The human being becomes a dividual:
divisible at will, analyzable, reconstructable – but without inner coherence.

2. The Dissolution of Responsibility

Without a stable self, there is no ethical responsibility.
Because responsibility presupposes that an agent remains the same over time –
that he or she makes decisions consciously, and can stand accountable for them as acts of freedom.

But if every action is ultimately determined by biochemical processes – as Harari implies –
then there is no freedom.
And without freedom, there is no guilt.

No remorse.
No repentance.
No moral choice.

In this worldview, the human being is no longer called to responsibility –
but to calculation.
Behavior is no longer an expression of one's inner disposition,
but the product of neural circuitry.

3. The Loss of Human Dignity

The idea of the inviolable dignity of every person – as expressed in Christianity or the Universal Declaration of Human Rights –
is based on the conviction that each human being possesses a unique, irreducible self.
A someone.
A being that cannot be replaced, exchanged, or instrumentalized,
because it carries within itself an unconditional worth.

But if that idea is replaced by the notion that the human is merely a temporary network of data flows,

then the person loses that inalienable value.
He or she becomes negotiable.
Usable.
Optimizable.
Erasable.

It is no coincidence that Harari openly suggests that humans may become obsolete in the future.
For in his thinking, the human is only relevant as long as he remains functional.
There is no inner reason for his existence.

4. The Slow Self-Abolition of Humanity

This view does not merely hollow out the individual –
it undermines the entire foundation of humanism.
If the human is no longer a subject but merely a calculable unit,
then concepts like freedom, conscience, maturity, or responsibility become empty metaphors –
useful for administration, but devoid of truth.

A society built on this worldview inevitably becomes technocratic, data-driven, instrumental.
And eventually, in Harari's own words,

"Man will no longer be needed."

This is not a dystopian fantasy.
It is the logical consequence of a view of the human being that denies the existence of an inner core.

And that is precisely why we must ask:

Is this view true?
Does it reflect the experience we have of ourselves?

4. A First Contrast – The Experience of the Self as Starting Point

There are many things we can doubt: opinions, memories, stories we've been told.
But there is one thing we cannot doubt without contradicting ourselves:

that we ourselves exist – as conscious beings, as experiencers, as "I am."

This immediate experience of one's own existence cannot be proven – and yet it cannot be denied.
It escapes all measurement and experimentation – and yet it is the foundation of all knowledge.
Whoever thinks – thinks.
Whoever experiences – experiences.
There is someone thinking.
There is someone experiencing.

Harari's model denies this dimension.
He reduces consciousness to the brain, the self to data processing, the subject to function.

But this reduction is only possible from the outside – never from within.
And that is the decisive difference:

A neuroscientist can measure brain activity – but cannot feel what a person feels when they love or suffer.

He can observe cognitive functions – but cannot grasp what it means to know oneself as an agent.

He can describe behavior – but cannot explain why someone freely chooses to act differently than they "should."

The subjectivity that Harari considers an illusion is, in truth, the first access point to reality.
Without it, there would be no philosophy, no ethics, no science –
because every one of these disciplines begins with a knowing subject.

The sentence "I am" is not a logical construction –

it is an experiential fact.
And it is unique, because it cannot be trans-
ferred outward.
Each human being experiences it only within.
And that is precisely the mark of their indi-
viduation – not their divisibility.

This experience – "I am" –
is the very point where Harari's view of humanity and the one we uphold ultimately
part ways:

For Harari, the self is a useful illusion, generated by evolutionary processes.

For us, the self is the origin of all truth –
that which remains when everything else
fades.

What one sees as deception,
the other sees as the gateway to reality.

This experience of the self cannot be proven

and yet it is the foundation of everything.
And it is not empty.
It bears traces.

It has depth.
It reaches toward its origin.

Who am I?
Why am I?
Where do I come from?
Where am I going?

These questions do not arise from the brain

they arise from the spirit.

Chapter 2 – Free Will as Illusion

Key Quote:

"Just as Christianity didn't disappear the day Darwin published On the Origin of Species, so liberalism won't vanish just because scientists have reached the conclusion that there are no free individuals."

(Yuval Noah Harari, Homo Deus: A Brief History of Tomorrow)

At first glance, this sentence may sound casual—almost ironic.
But it contains one of the most radical assertions in Harari's entire body of thought:

The human being has no free will.

Everything we perceive as choice, intuition, or decision is, in his model, the result of biological and psychological processes over which we have no real control.

The consequence:

Not only the classical image of the human being, but also the foundations of humanism, democracy, law, and ethics are called into question.

For if there are no "free individuals," as Harari claims—

then who decides?

Who acts?

Who bears responsibility?

As in the previous chapter, we will proceed by unfolding the logic of his position in four parts:

Part 1: What Harari Says – and What He Means

We examine the quote in context, clarify the meaning of the formulation, and show how it amounts to a comprehensive attack on the concept of free will.

Part 2: The Premises – Neuroscientific Determinism

We explore the scientific (and purportedly scientific) foundations of Harari's denial of freedom: neurology, psychology, behavior theory—and the philosophical assumptions embedded within them.

Part 3: The Consequences – The Collapse of Humanism
What happens when the idea of free will falls? What are the implications for society, morality, law, and responsibility? And what does Harari propose in its place?

Part 4: Freedom as Reality – And Why It Is Needed
We argue that freedom is not an illusion but a lived reality—and that every act of speech, every choice, every ethical stance depends on it.
The human being is not free because he "imagines it,"

but because he is.

1. What Harari Says – and What He Means

Harari's thesis:

"Just as Christianity didn't disappear the day Darwin published On the Origin of Species, so liberalism won't vanish just because scientists have reached the conclusion that there are no free individuals."

At first glance, this statement seems almost offhanded – like a passing remark.
Yet it contains a concentrated ideological message whose full implications are easily overlooked:
Harari declares that human free will has been scientifically disproven –
and at the same time, he notes that our societies are not yet ready to accept this fact.

The comparison with Christianity is no accident.
Harari points to the moment when Darwin's theory of evolution shook the theological view of man.
Now he draws a parallel:

71

Just as belief in God was relativized by natural science, so too is belief in human freedom being undermined by neuroscience.

The punchline:
Even if liberalism continues to exist,
its foundation – the free individual – can no longer be upheld scientifically.

What exactly is Harari claiming?

That there are no free individuals.
According to Harari, human beings do not act out of inner freedom, but according to causes they do not control: genes, upbringing, brain chemistry, social conditioning.
What we perceive as choice is merely the product of processes that lie outside our conscious control.

That this is a scientific finding.
Harari appeals to neuroscience, particularly to studies claiming to show that the brain initiates decisions before they are registered by consciousness.
From this, he concludes:

Free will is an illusion – a story we tell ourselves to retrospectively justify our behavior.

That our social systems are based on an illusion.
Democracy, law, ethics, education – all presuppose that humans are capable of making free decisions and acting responsibly.
But if that is not the case, then – in Harari's view – these are outdated constructs that will not withstand the test of time.

What lies between the lines?

Harari does not say that freedom is "morally wrong" –

he says it does not exist.
And that is far more radical.

Because if there is no freedom, then the human being is not a subject,
but an object –
steered, predictable, controllable.
And ultimately: manipulable.

This idea becomes fertile ground for techno-cratic systems:
If humans are not free, they can be guided.
If they are merely algorithms, they can be optimized.

The sentence Harari formulates sounds calm
–
but it carries explosive force.
It is not merely an opinion,
but a worldview:

one in which the human being no longer belongs to himself.

2. The Premises – Neuroscientific Determinism

The claim that free will is an illusion is not merely Harari's personal opinion.
It rests on a specific scientific framework: neuroscientific determinism.
This model assumes that all mental, emotional, and volitional processes are fully explainable by measurable events in the brain – and therefore ultimately determined, that is: predetermined.

Harari draws on key arguments that gained popularity in recent decades through neurobiological studies.
At the center of this discussion stands an experiment that has been widely debated since the 1980s:

the research conducted by Benjamin Libet, which showed that certain electrical activities in the brain (so-called readiness potentials) occur before a conscious decision to act is registered.

Libet himself was cautious in his interpretation – he spoke of a "veto right" of consciousness.

But later researchers – and popular interpreters like Harari – drew a far more radical conclusion:

If the brain decides before the mind is aware of it,

then the will is not free – it is merely a commentary after the fact.

The assumptions underlying this view:

All thinking is brain activity.

There is no "mind" in the metaphysical sense, but only physically measurable processes: electrical impulses, chemical reactions, synaptic wiring.

Every decision is causally explainable.

What appears to be choice is in fact the result of complex cause-and-effect chains: genetic predisposition, past experience, environment, current biochemical state.

Consciousness is a secondary effect.

What we perceive as a "decision" is the act of an internal observer who rationalizes what has already occurred – without actually steering it.

These assumptions may seem plausible at first – especially because they are based on empirical data.
But they rest on a methodological reductionism that elevates one form of thinking to an absolute:

Only what can be measured is considered real.

That means:

Experiences, intentions, questions of meaning, conscience – all of these are not considered "wrong," but epiphenomenal: byproducts without causal relevance.

And this is precisely the point Harari picks up:

If the brain explains everything, there is no need for a self.

If processes determine everything, there is no need for freedom.
If algorithms can predict human behavior better than the person himself –
what role remains for subjective choice?

A seemingly objective claim – with an ideological edge

What is presented as scientific progress is, upon closer inspection, not an empirical proof,
but an interpretation – shaped by a materialist philosophy that regards as real only what can be externally observed, measured, repeated, and calculated.

This way of thinking ignores – or at least relativizes – the first-person perspective:
the direct experience of choice, decision, and responsibility.
It cannot access this inner space of consciousness – and thus concludes that it is not real.

But as we will see in Part 4,

it is precisely this inner experience that is not only real,

but the foundation of all ethics, communication, and spiritual orientation.

Before that, however, we turn in the next section to the logical and social consequences of Harari's rejection of freedom.

3. The Collapse of Humanism

The denial of free will, as put forward by Harari, is not merely an attack on a philosophical concept.
If taken seriously, it amounts to the end of humanism.

For what is humanism at its core?

It is the conviction that the human being is a free and rational subject.
That he can shape himself and the world –
within the bounds of moral responsibility.
That he is an end in himself, not a means.
And that he, as such, is the bearer of dignity, rights, and freedom –
independent of utility or function.

All of this rests on a single foundational assumption:

Man can will. And he can will otherwise.

But if we follow Harari's reasoning –
that every decision, every act of willing, every form of behavior is the inevitable

product of prior conditions – biological, chemical, social –
then this assumption no longer holds.

What collapses with freedom?
Responsibility
Without freedom, there is no ethical responsibility.
No one is "responsible" in the moral sense if they could not have acted otherwise.
Guilt, remorse, forgiveness – all of this loses meaning if the perpetrator is not a subject, but merely the result of a chain of events.

Justice
Legal systems are built on the assumption that people can choose between alternatives –

that they decide, and in doing so either uphold or violate norms.
But if every action is ultimately determined, punishment becomes arbitrary – or purely preventative, functional, and deterrent.
The human being is no longer judged for what he is, but for what he does – and soon, only for what he might do.

Education

Education presupposes that people can develop – not just cognitively, but morally, spiritually, and personally.

But if all development is merely adaptation to neural processes,

then education becomes behavioral conditioning.

Pedagogy loses its spiritual dimension and becomes a technology.

Morality

All morality depends on the possibility of choice.

If there are no alternatives to action, there can be no good or evil – only efficiency, usefulness, adaptation.

Ethics degenerates into statistics and risk management.

Man as Problem and Project

Harari does not elaborate on these consequences polemically –

but they are implicit in his thinking.

If the human being is no longer a free being, then he also loses his special status.

He is no longer a goal –

but a transitional stage, a temporary project
on the path toward something else:
machines, algorithms, superior systems.

What quietly disappears in the process is the
idea of man as a bearer of meaning.
If man is not free, then he is also not responsible –
and thus, no longer significant.
He is reduced to what he can functionally
contribute.
And if machines can do it better,
then, as Harari puts it – simply and coolly –

the human being becomes obsolete.

Humanism does not die by an attack from
outside.

It dies when its foundations are denied from
within – and no one objects.

But is the human being truly unfree?
Or is it rather science that misunderstands its
own limits?

4. Freedom as Reality – And Why It Is Needed

The idea that free will is an illusion may, at first, sound "scientifically sober" – almost modern, progressive, even liberating.
But anyone who follows this thought to its conclusion quickly realizes:

A world without freedom is no longer a world for human beings.

Without freedom, everything that defines the human person –
responsibility, conscience, love, remorse, meaning, guilt, vocation –
becomes nothing but deception.
Harari's vision of a "post-human" world begins at the very point where the human being ceases to belong to himself.

But is this true?
Is freedom merely a subjective feeling –
or is it a real fact, which may not be measurable, but can nonetheless be experienced and understood?

1. Freedom cannot be proven – but it can be experienced
No one can "prove" freedom empirically.
It does not show up in blood tests, nor on a brain scan, nor in statistical models.
But that does not mean it does not exist – on the contrary:

Freedom is a fact of inner experience – just like consciousness, thought, or identity.

We know we are free –
not because someone told us,
but because we experience it.

We can decide. We can reflect.
We can resist our impulses.
We can change ourselves.
We can reorient our lives.

We feel the tension between option A and option B.
We struggle with ourselves.
We wrestle with what is right.

Whoever knows this struggle, knows they are free.

2. Freedom is the condition of all responsibility

Without freedom, no one can be held accountable.
No judge, no teacher, no educator, no therapist, no priest, no friend can take a person seriously

if that person could not have acted differently.

Only a free human being can respond –
to themselves,
to others,
to God.

And that is what responsibility means:

the ability to respond.

This ability is not the byproduct of biochemistry –
it is the expression of the human being's spiritual nature.
Without it, the human being is nothing but a reactive machine – not a personal being.

3. Freedom is the space in which the good becomes possible

Freedom is not arbitrariness.
It is not "doing whatever I want."
True freedom means choosing the good –
even when evil is possible.

It is the space in which the human being can transcend himself – not automatically, but consciously.

Harari ignores this space.
For him, the human being is a function-bearer – driven, not sovereign.

But reality tells a different story:
Human beings choose against power, against instinct, against fear –
out of love, conviction, truth.

This freedom is real.
And it is essential –
not just for the individual, but for every society that wishes to rest on human dignity, law, and moral responsibility.

4. Freedom points beyond itself

Where does freedom come from?
Why does it exist – even though it is uncomfortable, paradoxical, even dangerous?

This question leads beyond the boundaries of science.
For freedom cannot be derived from matter.
No stone, no plant, no animal is truly free.
Only the human being asks, decides, chooses
–
and in doing so, becomes self-aware.

Freedom is the sign that the human being is not merely nature – but spirit.

And spirit – like consciousness itself – cannot be explained from within the world,
but points beyond the world.

It is here that the path opens to a deeper understanding of the human being –
and to the question of whether there is an origin from which this freedom arises.

But before we step fully onto that path,
we turn in Chapter 3 to a third pillar of human existence –

and how it, too, is dismantled by Harari:

Meaning.

Chapter 3 – The Denial of Meaning

Key Quote:

"As far as we can tell, from a purely scientific viewpoint, human life has absolutely no meaning. Humans are the outcome of blind evolutionary processes that operate without goal or purpose. Our actions are not part of some divine cosmic plan, and if planet Earth were to blow up tomorrow morning, the universe would probably keep going about its business as usual. As far as we can tell at this point, human subjectivity would not be missed. Hence any meaning that people ascribe to their lives is just a delusion."

(Yuval Noah Harari, jewishreviewofbooks.com + wikiquote.org)

Few quotes express Harari's worldview as clearly and starkly as this one.
He does not merely state that the universe contains no inherent meaning –

he declares every form of meaning that humans assign to their lives to be an illusion.

What remains is a worldview of cosmic indifference – cold, empty, functional.

With this, Harari moves beyond scientific description into the realm of existential interpretation.
And this is precisely where our analysis begins.
Because behind this seemingly sober statement lies more than mere observation of nature –

it is the expression of a metaphysical nihilism that presents itself as "objective,"
but in truth reflects a profound ideological choice.

As in the previous chapters, we will proceed in four steps:

Part 1: What Harari Says – and What He Means
We analyze the quote sentence by sentence.

What does it really mean to say that "all meaning is illusion"?
And how does Harari justify this claim?

Part 2: The Premises – Metaphysical Nihilism
We show that Harari's denial of meaning is not the result of scientific necessity,
but of a philosophical decision: the exclusion of all transcendence.

Part 3: The Consequences – Cosmic Indifference as Worldview
What does a life without meaning entail?
What happens to a person who sees himself as meaningless?
And what unfolds when entire cultures adopt this worldview?

Part 4: Why Meaning Is Not an Illusion
We show that meaning is not something we fabricate –
but something we discover.
That human beings do not "invent," but respond.
And that meaning always points to something greater than ourselves –

something that is not indifferent.

1. What Harari Says – and What He Means

Harari's Thesis:

"As far as we can tell from a purely scientific viewpoint, human life has absolutely no meaning. Humans are the outcome of blind evolutionary processes that operate without goal or purpose. Our actions are not part of some divine cosmic plan, and if the planet were to blow up tomorrow morning, the universe would probably keep going about its business as usual. As far as we can tell at this point, human subjectivity would not be missed. Hence, any meaning people ascribe to their lives is just a delusion."

At this point, Harari is no longer speaking about history, technology, or politics –
he is speaking about the meaning of life.
And his answer is as clear as it is absolute:

There is none.

He does not argue – he declares.
He offers no uncertainty – only a diagnosis:

The human being is an accident of evolution, and every attempt to ascribe meaning to life is self-deception.

Analysis of the Quote – Sentence by Sentence

"As far as we can tell from a purely scientific viewpoint, human life has absolutely no meaning."

This opening sentence is both thesis and frame.
Harari explicitly refers to the "scientific viewpoint" –
as if science were qualified to make definitive judgments about meaning.
What sounds like an objective statement is, in fact, a displacement of responsibility:
It is not Harari who says this – it is "science."
Or more precisely: as far as we can tell.

The problem is this:
Science can describe processes, analyze structures, uncover causes –
but it cannot measure metaphysical meaning.

What is presented here as a scientific result
is actually a philosophical conclusion
based on a materialist worldview.

*"Humans are the outcome of blind evolution-
ary processes that operate without goal or
purpose."*

This statement repeats Darwin's biological
perspective,
but adds a metaphysical negation: "without
goal or purpose."
Yet this is not an empirical fact –
it is an interpretation of evolutionary theory,
not its necessary consequence.

One could just as plausibly say:
Human beings are the result of an intentional
creative process unfolding through evolution.
The data remain the same – only the interpretation differs.

*"Our actions are not part of some divine cos-
mic plan."*

Again, Harari does not simply doubt religion

he replaces it entirely.
He rejects not just a particular idea of God,
but any form of transcendental framework.
This is not a cautious "we don't know."
It is a blunt: "There is no plan. Period."

"And if the planet were to blow up tomorrow morning, the universe would probably keep going about its business as usual."

This sentence borders on cynical – but it is consistent.
It expresses the worldview that results when all metaphysical meaning is denied:
The universe is indifferent.
It does not react.
It does not remember.
It does not miss.

In this vision, the human being is not the center,
not the crown, not the steward –
but a passing byproduct.

"As far as we can tell at this point, human subjectivity would not be missed."

Perhaps the most brutal sentence in the entire quote.
It denies not only the dignity of the individual,
but the very legitimacy of human existence.

Subjectivity – the ability to feel, to love, to hope, to believe –
is irrelevant in this worldview.
Whether it exists or not –

it makes no difference.

"Hence, any meaning people ascribe to their lives is just a delusion."

And here is the final thesis:
Not only is there no objective meaning –
even subjective meaning is dismissed as illusion.

Love, vocation, sacrifice, hope, religion, art, truth –

all of it: illusion.

What Harari Means

Harari is not building a new theory –
he is drawing the final consequence of a
worldview based entirely on
matter, function, and cause-effect logic.

He gives voice to what remains unspoken in
many modern philosophies:

The human being has no deeper ground.
No meaning.
No answer.

But he says it with the authority of "science"
and with the calm tone of a "rational observer."

What Is Overlooked

This view is not neutral.
It is not mere description –
it is a position, a decision.
And it has consequences.
For the individual.
For culture.
For life itself.

2. The Premises – Metaphysical Nihilism

Yuval Noah Harari claims that life has no objective meaning.
He asserts that human beings are the product of blind, purposeless processes.
Any attempt to assign meaning to life, he says, is an illusion.

But these statements are not the result of scientific proof.
They stem from a specific metaphysical stance that Harari assumes, but does not justify: nihilism.

More precisely: a metaphysical nihilism that excludes not only God,
but every transcendent dimension of being from the outset.

1. What Is Metaphysical Nihilism?
It is the conviction that there are no objective values, no higher purpose, no final cause,
and no transcendent reference point.
Everything that exists is immanent movement without direction.

What we experience as "meaning" is a psychological projection – not a metaphysical reality.

This stance is fundamentally different from mere atheism.

An atheist does not believe in God –
but may still acknowledge meaning, ethics, or spiritual depth in human life.

A metaphysical nihilist, on the other hand, denies any and all ultimate significance.

He accepts no spiritual dimension, no foundation of being, no teleological structure, no source of consciousness – nothing beyond what is measurable and functional.

2. Harari's Core Assumption: Everything Can Be Explained – and Nothing Has Meaning
Harari adopts the position of radical naturalism:

The human being is fully explicable through natural processes.

Meaning arises exclusively in the brain – as a by-product of evolution.

Meaning is a "useful error" – helpful for social cohesion, but without ontological depth.

This perspective has not been disproven – but neither has it been proven.

It is an interpretive framework, not a logical consequence of science.
Yet Harari presents it as the only reasonable worldview – because it seems "realistic."

3. Why This Nihilism Is a Choice
No one can empirically demonstrate that life has no meaning.

The question of meaning goes beyond the methods of empirical science –
it is not about the what, but the why.

Anyone seeking to answer it must argue philosophically or religiously –
not biologically or statistically.

So when Harari claims there is no meaning, he does so because:

he excludes any transcendent dimension from the start;

he regards every spiritual experience as self-deception;

and he interprets world events solely as a random process without direction.

But this is not "objective." It is a position. And it is a choice.

4. The Result: A Closed Worldview – Without Exit

Harari operates within a fully immanent co-ordinate system.
Everything that points to something "higher" – whether God, spirit, truth, or vocation – is dismissed as myth.

This is not an open worldview.
It is a closed system that:

devalues all deeper questions;

relativizes all subjective experience;

and replaces any hope for meaning with the label "illusion."

Conclusion

Harari's denial of meaning is not the result of scientific discovery.

It is the expression of a metaphysical nihilism that dismisses what it cannot prove – and thus assumes it does not exist.

But this nihilism is not a neutral worldview.

It has consequences – for the individual, for culture, and for humanity itself.

3. Cosmic Indifference as a Worldview

Harari presents himself as a sober observer of the world.
But what he actually outlines is an existential worldview—a vision of the universe in which the human being plays no role whatsoever.
Not a central one, not a symbolic one, not even a marginal one.

In his perspective, the universe is neither hostile nor benevolent—it is simply indifferent.
And this indifference is not an empirical observation, but the backdrop against which every human hope is reduced to mere projection.

1. A Disenchanted Cosmos
For Harari, there is no "above," no "beyond," no "why."

The universe was not created.

It follows no plan.

It responds to nothing—not to suffering, not to love, not to longing.

Human beings are not the "crown of creation" in this view, but the accidental result of cosmic processes, falsely convinced of their own significance.
And this misconception, Harari argues, is a biological strategy:
Humans had to invent meaning in order to remain functional.

In reality, he writes, "our subjectivity would not be missed" if we disappeared tomorrow.
The universe would carry on—without us.

2. A Worldview of Emptiness
This kind of thinking is not progress—it is a spiritual regression.
It robs life of its depth, suffering of its meaning, and love of its foundation.
Anything that cannot be measured, used, or technically harnessed is quietly devalued.

In such a worldview:

Death is nothing more than the end of function.

Birth is a biological event without calling.

History is not a drama, but an algorithm in motion.

One can still function within such a worldview—
but no longer hope as a human being.

3. The Psychological Consequence: Uprootedness
A person who sees themselves as meaningless can respond in only two ways:

They numb themselves—with distraction, consumption, entertainment, speed.

Or they harden themselves—with cynicism, technocratic belief, control.

In both cases, they lose their inner connection to what actually defines them:
The sense that their life has a meaning—
not imposed from outside,

but arising from a depth that is both beyond them and intimately tied to them.

Harari's worldview declares this depth irrelevant.
For him, there is no "inner calling," no "longing," no "answer from transcendence."
Everything is silent. And this silence, to him, is the truth.

But for the human soul, it means this:
Uprootedness, isolation, abandonment.

4. The Cultural Consequence: Meaninglessness as a System
If this worldview becomes the foundation of education, politics, science, and society—what remains?

Why still make sacrifices?

Why still take responsibility?

Why still ask questions—if every answer is an illusion?

Such a worldview cannot sustain a culture.

It can organize systems, manage processes, control behavior—
but it cannot generate meaning.
It cannot say what humans live for, or where they are going.

Harari accepts this—almost calmly.
But for the cultural history of humanity, it would be a rupture:

For the first time, the human being would stand in a world that no longer responds.

And worse still:

He would be convinced this is a good thing.

But is meaning truly an illusion?
Or does the very fact that the human being asks about meaning point to its reality?

4. Why Meaning Is Not an Illusion

Yuval Noah Harari claims:

"Every meaning that humans assign to their lives is an illusion."

Yet this—despite all apparent scientific sobriety—is a claim that runs against experience. Because human beings experience meaning. They do not search for it simply because they need a story—
they search because they are responding to something that touches them.

Meaning is not invented.
It is discovered.

1. Meaning as Experience—Not Construction
When a person says:

"My life has meaning,"

they do not mean:

"I've made up a story."

They mean:

"I sense that my life is embedded in a larger context—something that reaches beyond me, and yet includes me."

This experience cannot be proven—
but it is no less real than hunger, pain, or joy.

It is a spiritual perception—
not material, but real.

Human beings are the only creatures who ask:
"Why?"
And the only beings who suffer from the absence of meaning.

That alone shows:
Meaning is not illusion—
it is a dimension of being human.

2. Meaning Has a Source—Not a Cause
What Harari overlooks is this:

Meaning is not the result of neural activity—
it is what transcends it.

A person can find meaning in suffering—
even when nothing outwardly improves.

A person can assign meaning to a life that has
failed by all external measures—
because they perceive something beyond
the visible.

Meaning is not function.
It is response—
to a call that does not come from within, but
reaches the person from beyond.

Whoever has felt this knows:

"That was not me. That was something
greater than me—and yet within me."

3. Meaning Is Universal—And Yet Personal

All the great cultures of humanity—from antiquity to Christianity to Eastern mysticism—
did not produce meaning.
They searched for it.

They were convinced:

That life is not empty.

That the human being is called.

That behind existence lies a source—not in-different, but responsive.

This search is not over.
It begins anew in every person who asks:

Why am I here?

What am I living for?

Where does my longing come from?

Such questions cannot be silenced.
And they cannot be answered by the word "illusion."

Only those who already believe that meaning must not exist will deny it.

4. Meaning Points to the One Who Gives It
If we do not create the meaning of our lives—
but discover it—
then another question arises:

Who placed it there?

Who calls us—when we feel called?

The reality of meaning contradicts what Harari claims—
not ideologically, but existentially.

The question of meaning cannot be answered with statistics or molecules—
because it is a question that rises from the depths of the human being.

Whoever hears it knows it is not imagined.
And whoever follows it senses:
It seeks a response.

This is the threshold where Harari's thinking is most fully revealed—
not because his reasoning is flawed,
but because he systematically excludes what is deeply human.

And so, in a final step of this chapter, we take a closer look at what Harari presents as "neutral"—

and what, on closer inspection, reveals itself
as an implicit agenda.

5. Why Harari Is Not Neutral—But Follows an Ideological Agenda

Yuval Noah Harari presents himself as a sober analyst. His language is calm, his tone seemingly objective, his reasoning built with logical precision. He references scientific studies, avoids polemics, and insists he is merely describing reality—not prescribing how things ought to be.

But this is exactly where the deception lies.

Harari is not neutral. He does not merely describe—he judges, asserts, and negates. And he does so from within a worldview that does not emerge from science itself, but from a rigorously applied—yet unacknowledged—materialism, which excludes everything spiritual, transcendent, or personal a priori.

1. The Ideology of Disenchantment

Harari assumes that all forms of meaning, freedom, soul, and self-consciousness are illusions—products of evolutionary utility, not of truth. This conviction runs through his entire thinking like an underground current:

Religion, for him, is a useful "fiction."

Morality, an evolutionary control mechanism.

History, a narrative of shifting power structures.

Love, hope, and vocation are biochemical strategies.

None of this is a neutral observation—
it is an ideological decision.

He could interpret the same biological data differently:
As signs of a spiritual reality,
as the unfolding of a consciousness in relation to a greater whole.

But Harari chooses not to.
And he does so without acknowledging that it is a choice.

2. The Strategy: Science as Authority—Without Methodological Reflection

Harari repeatedly appeals to the "scientific view."
But he fails to reflect on the fact that science cannot make metaphysical judgments—
it can describe how we perceive meaning in the brain,
but not whether meaning exists.

Harari leverages the authority of science—but oversteps its methodological boundaries.
He confuses description with interpretation, data with existence, function with truth.

The result is a system that creates the illusion of objectivity—
but is in fact built upon an unspoken worldview:

Whatever cannot be calculated is meaningless.

Whatever cannot be measured is irrelevant.

Whatever is not functional is an illusion.

3. The Effect: Emptiness in the Name of Enlightenment

Harari's worldview is not just theory—it has consequences.

It shapes patterns of thought, education, media, culture.

It gives many people the feeling of being "enlightened"
as they distance themselves from traditional ideas—
without realizing that they are not being liberated,
but emptied.

Because:

Whoever believes that life has no meaning does not become free—they become abandoned.

Whoever believes they are not a free subject does not become rational—they become manipulable.

Whoever believes the self is an illusion does not become objective—they become invisible.

Harari's thinking is not a cold mirror of reality.
It is a systematic worldview—one that ultimately leads to the abolition of the human being in the name of enlightenment.

With this final step, the picture is complete.

We have taken Harari's ideas seriously.
We did not fight them—we examined them.
We listened—
and we took him at his word.

And that is what has shown us:

What appears as progress is, in truth, retreat.

And what masquerades as sobriety is, in fact, disenchantment.

But Harari does not stop at theory.
As we will see in the coming chapters:

He develops from this a system designed to replace the human being technologically—all while claiming to serve them.

Chapter 4 – The New God Is Called Algorithm

1. Dataism as a Replacement for Religion

At the center of Yuval Noah Harari's vision of the future stands a concept that he either coined or at least significantly popularized: Dataism.
It is a worldview no longer founded on God, spirit, or meaning—but on information, data flows, and algorithmic efficiency.

For Harari, Dataism is more than just a technical paradigm—he describes it as a new universal religion, one that supersedes the old narratives.

"If you see data flow as the highest value, then a new ethic emerges:
Whatever enhances the flow of data is good.
Whatever obstructs it is bad."
(paraphrased from Homo Deus)

What Is Dataism?
Dataism holds that:

The universe is a data-processing system,

All organisms are essentially algorithms,

And the highest value lies in the efficiency of information flow.

In other words:
The human being is no longer at the center—
data processing itself is.

The value of a living being is measured by its ability to receive, process, and transmit information.

In this logic:

The body becomes a sensor,

The brain becomes an interface,

Consciousness becomes a redundant by-product.

What matters is no longer the experience—
but the capacity to compute.

From Humanism to Dataism
Harari narrates the intellectual history of the West as a succession of dominant worldviews:

Theocentric – with God at the center,

Anthropocentric – with man at the center,

Datacentric – with information at the center.

In this narrative, Dataism appears not as a threat, but as the next stage of progress.

He speaks of humanism in the past tense and paints a future in which the human being is replaced by systems that calculate better, predict better, control better—and therefore decide better.

How Does Dataism Mirror Religion?
Harari himself draws multiple parallels between classical religion and Dataism:

Classical Religion
God as highest authority
Prayer, meditation

Revelation
Faith
Sin

vs.

Dataism
Algorithm as highest authority
Input, interface
Output, prediction
Trust in computation
Data loss, system error

In this system, the human being is no longer seen as sacred,
but as a temporary data processor, soon to be replaced by more efficient systems.

And that is where the religious structure becomes clear:

There is a higher order (data flow),
a supreme good (efficiency),
and a hope of salvation (optimization through technology).

What Gets Lost in the Process?

In this new "faith":

There is no soul,

No vocation,

No free will,

No transcendent meaning.

There are only systems and their functionality.
The human is no longer a seeker of truth, but a conduit of signals.

Harari describes all this coldly and precisely—but not with detachment.
He admires this development.
He sees it as inevitable—and historically necessary.

But what does this mean, concretely, for the human being?

2. The Human as Data Point – Evaluation, Surveillance, Control

If the highest good is no longer freedom, truth, or dignity,
but rather the efficiency of data flow,
then everything changes:

The role of the human being,
their value to society,
their self-understanding—
and above all, the degree to which systems gain access to their inner and outer life.

In Harari's thinking, the human is no longer conceived as a subject,
but as a node in a network of information.
Not a bearer of consciousness,
but a sensor,
whose task is to produce data—and to allow themselves to be constantly optimized in the process.

1. From Citizen to Data Set
In a dataistic system, the human being becomes increasingly digitized:

their thoughts (search queries, likes, posts)

their emotions (emojis, chat histories, vocal patterns)

their behavior (GPS tracking, purchase history, movement profiles)

their bodily functions (wearables, medical sensors)

Everything is collected, evaluated, stored, and processed.

What matters is not who you are,
but how much data you generate—and how "useful" that data is to the system.

The human being loses their uniqueness—
and becomes a data point in the stream of algorithmic evaluation.

2. Evaluation: The New Moral Code
In a data-driven society, a new form of morality emerges—
or rather: a new system of value assignment.

No longer do conscience, ethics, or virtue decide—
but algorithms that evaluate behavior.

This is not a hypothetical development—
it is already becoming reality:

Credit scores are calculated algorithmically.

Job applications are filtered by data profiles.

Social networks reward visibility, conformity, engagement—not truth.

What unfolds is a subtle normalization of the human being:

You are no longer punished—you are downgraded.
You are no longer heard—you are de-algorithmized.

3. Surveillance: Transparency Without a Subject
Harari openly states that modern technologies "know us better than we know ourselves."

He describes—half in warning, half in awe—
how Big Data can detect feelings, decisions,
and even diseases before the individual is
aware of them.

Yet his analysis remains technical, not ethical.

He does not ask:

Who has access?

Who decides what is seen?

What happens to those who opt out?

Because in Harari's worldview, there is no ultimate responsibility.
If there is no free will, then surveillance is not
a moral concern—
only a question of efficiency.

And that opens the door to a new kind of totality:
not through violence,
but through systemic transparency.

4. Control: Behavior Instead of Conviction
If the human is no longer a free subject,
then there is no need to persuade—only to
steer.

The tools:

Recommendation algorithms

Nudging (behavioral steering via interface
design)

Constant feedback

Automated consequences

The political utopia of modernity was:
Enlightenment through education.

The techno-utopian reality is:
Behavioral control through data.

Harari does not describe this as dystopia—
but as the next logical step:

A system that knows what you want before
you do—

and guides you toward where you'll "func-tion efficiently."

What used to be conscience is now a feed-back loop.

What used to be dialogue is now a filter bub-ble.

What used to be the human becomes an op-timized interface.

And those who are no longer needed—are replaced.

3. The Replacement of Consciousness by Function – Harari's New Paradigm

"Until today, high intelligence always went hand in hand with a developed consciousness. ... However, we are now developing new types of non-conscious intelligence that can perform such tasks far better than humans. ... This raises a novel question: which of the two is really important, intelligence or consciousness?"

(Yuval Noah Harari, Homo Deus: A History of Tomorrow)

With this quote, Harari formulates one of the most consequential thoughts in his entire body of work: Consciousness is no longer seen as essential—only optional.

Throughout history, intelligence and consciousness have always appeared together—embodied in the thinking, feeling, and morally responsible human being. But now, in our technocratic modernity, a new category emerges: intelligence without consciousness.

AI systems that calculate efficiently—but do not feel.

That solve problems—but have no intentions.

That compute—but do not comprehend.

And here's the twist: Harari asks which of the two is ultimately more important.

In doing so—without directly stating it—he places consciousness on the chopping block. And that, behind all the rhetorical restraint, represents a civilizational rupture. For it implies nothing less than the hollowing out of what it means to be human—in favor of more efficient, non-conscious machinery.

The False Dilemma

But the alternative Harari presents—intelligence or consciousness—is fundamentally flawed.

Intelligence without consciousness can only produce what it is programmed to do.
It has no impulse of its own.
No aim.
No question.

No "why."

Only consciousness carries intention.
Only a conscious being can want something,
pursue an idea, ask a question, or perceive a
problem that hasn't yet been defined.
Without consciousness, intelligence is like an
engine running in idle: powerful, but point-
less.
Every action of a non-conscious system remains reactive—never creative.

Why Consciousness Comes First
What Harari ignores—or deliberately
omits—is the first-person perspective that
underlies all thinking and understanding.
I am—and because I am, I can want, question, judge, and decide.

This "I am" consciousness is not merely a by-
product of neural activity.
It is the bearer of all meaning, all ethics, and
all spiritual structure.

A system might solve problems better than a
human—but it knows nothing about it.
It experiences nothing.

It wants nothing.
It does not exist.

Without consciousness, there is no subject—
and without a subject, there is no world.

Life and Consciousness – Two Sides of One
Reality
At this point, a deeper connection becomes
visible.
Life itself is always intentional.
A living being strives—it resists, adapts,
evolves.
Life is never just a mechanical process.
It is oriented existence.

And the same applies to consciousness: it is
not passive, but directed, inquisitive, per-
ceiving.

To live is to will. To will is to be conscious.

From this arises a powerful insight:

Life and consciousness are not separate phenomena.

They are two expressions of the same spiritual reality—
the reality of personal existence.

They cannot emerge from dead matter.
And they cannot be replaced by mere function.

Harari's Blind Spot
That Harari overlooks this fundamental truth
is not due to lack of intelligence—
but to a foundational misconception:

He confuses performance with meaning.

Because machines are becoming more intelligent,
he believes they can replace humans.

But machines do not live—
they only function.

This reveals the core error in Harari's thinking:

He assumes that the question "What works better?" can replace the question "What is?"

But that is not the case.

Intelligence without consciousness is not the future of humanity.
It is merely the next stage of technology.

What remains is the old truth:

Only one who is conscious can will.
Only one who wills can act.
Only one who acts is truly human.

And it is precisely what Harari considers dispensable
that is the sole reason history, culture, and a future exist at all.

4. The Utopia of the Redundant Human

Perhaps the most far-reaching idea in all of Harari's work is this: that human beings—or at least large portions of humanity—could soon become redundant.

And by "redundant," he doesn't mean inconvenient or difficult to integrate.
He means: no longer needed.

"Humans are not equal. The difference between them will grow in the future. As machines improve, the vast majority of humans will have nothing to offer that is competitive."

(Paraphrased from Homo Deus)

1. The "Useless Class"
Harari openly speaks of a future social class he calls the "useless class."

It consists of people who:

are displaced from the job market by AI and automation,

can no longer be "retrained" by traditional education systems,

and fulfill no function in the techno-economic system.

He argues that this development cannot be fixed through retraining or redistribution—because algorithms learn faster, work more reliably, are cheaper, and require no rest, motivation, or ethical consideration.

Thus, the human being as a laborer becomes obsolete. And in Harari's logic, this isn't a tragic accident—
it's the next step in evolution.

2. Occupation Through Illusion
So what's to be done with these redundant humans?

Harari names two possibilities:

Biochemical control:
Drugs that regulate mood, stimulate drive, or manage apathy.
Virtual reality:

Simulations, games, artificial worlds where people can experience a sense of meaning—despite having none in the real world.

Harari himself compares this to the "Roman solution": bread and circuses.
Only now, not in the Colosseum—but in digital parallel realities.

Truth no longer matters—only function.
What matters is that the "useless class" remains quiet and doesn't disrupt the flow of data.

3. The New Übermensch: Tech-Elite + AI
While the masses are deemed "redundant," Harari envisions a technological elite with access to:

biotechnology,

neural enhancement,

artificial intelligence,

and cybernetic integration.

This gives rise to a new model of intelligence—or more precisely, a new model of what it means to be superior.

Homo sapiens is no longer seen as the end point of evolution, but merely as a temporary transitional form.

Harari says:

"In 300 years, Homo sapiens will not be the dominate life form on Earth, if we exist at all. ... The more likely possibility is that we will use bioengineering and machine learning and artificial intelligence either to upgrade ourselves into a totally different kind of being or to create a totally different kind of being that will take over. In any case, in 200 or 300 years, the beings that will dominate the Earth will be far more different from us than we are different from Neanderthals or from chimpanzees."

(www.vox.com, March 27, 2017 – Ezra Klein podcast)

So what remains of the human being, when others are smarter, more efficient, and permanently superior?

We are no longer needed—
and perhaps no longer wanted.

4. Dehumanization as a Logical Outcome
These ideas sound radical—but they follow logically from Harari's foundational premises:

If humans have no free will,

no soul,

no objective dignity,

if consciousness is merely an epiphenomenon,

and meaning is an illusion—

then the human being is nothing that needs to be protected.
He is merely a function—or a malfunction.

In this worldview, the "utopia of the redundant human" is not a horror.
It's an increase in efficiency.

And that's exactly what makes it so dangerous:

Because it doesn't scream.
Because it doesn't threaten.
Because it presents itself as the rational outcome of progress—
while erasing the human in the process.

Chapter 5 – A Contradiction in Itself

1. How Harari's System Undermines Itself

Yuval Noah Harari claims that the human being is not an individual.

He denies the self, free will, and any form of objective meaning. According to him, the human is a "dividual"—a fleeting, process-based formation of biochemical activity. Nothing enduring, nothing substantial.

But with this assertion, Harari doesn't just undermine human dignity or the ideals of humanism—
he undermines himself.

Because:

If there is no "I" – who is speaking?

If the self is nothing but an illusion, then the speaker is also an illusion.
If freedom does not exist, then the decision to write a book is not a real decision.

If meaning is merely deception, then every statement is meaningless—including Harari's own.

In other words:

If Harari were right, there would be no one who could say what he says.

This is the point where his entire intellectual system collapses in on itself:
It produces statements about the world—while simultaneously denying that there is a subject who can make statements.

A form of thinking that denies thought itself.
A speaker who denies his own existence—in the very act of speaking.
A system that doesn't just dehumanize—but disembodies.

2. The Performative Self-Contradiction of His Philosophy

In philosophy, a performative self-contradiction occurs when someone, through the act of speaking, does the opposite of what they are asserting.

Examples:

Someone who says, "I cannot speak," contradicts themselves—because they are speaking.

Someone who says, "There is no truth," is claiming a truth.

Someone who says, "No one can know anything," is claiming to know something.

This exact error lies at the heart of Harari's thinking—not occasionally, but structurally.

He says: "There is no self."
Yet he speaks as a self.

He says: "Free will is an illusion."

Yet he expresses convictions—as an act of free thought.

He says: "Life has no meaning."
Yet he wants to be understood—which presupposes meaning.

Every one of his statements lives off the opposite of what it claims.
Without a self—there is no speech.
Without freedom—there is no philosophy.
Without meaning—there is no communication.

Form Destroys Content

Harari writes books. He gives lectures. He gives interviews. He argues. He persuades.

All of this presupposes that there is:

someone who thinks,

someone who responds,

and someone who can be understood.

But his system says:

There is no thinker, no response, no understanding—only processes, impulses, and patterns.

His entire philosophy becomes a performative short-circuit.
It cannot exist if it is right.

The Blind Spot: Language as the Great Betrayer

Language betrays what the theory seeks to conceal.
Because in every sentence Harari writes, there is:

a subject,

an intentional assertion,

an addressee,

a claim to validity.

He cannot avoid this—because it is human.

Yet his philosophy denies exactly that humanity.

He wants to explain a world in which no one speaks—
and uses language to do so.

He wants to expose meaning—
and appeals to the reader's understanding.

He wants to abolish the self—
yet every thought he formulates begins from the self.

Conclusion of This Section:
Harari's philosophy cannot be thought, spoken, or written without contradicting itself.
It uses what it denies—and lives off what it seeks to abolish.

3. Why a World Without Self, Freedom, and Meaning Cannot Be Consistently Thought

Many things can be claimed. One can say there is no soul, no God, no ultimate purpose.
One can also say that the human being is merely biology, mere reaction, mere function.

But what one cannot say consistently is that:

there is no self,

no freedom,

and no meaning

while simultaneously expecting that this claim will be heard, understood, or even accepted.

Because:

A world without self, freedom, and meaning is not only inhuman—it is unthinkable.

1. Why a Self Is Necessary to Think

Every thought presupposes a thinking subject.

One cannot think without thinking that one thinks.

This "I think" is not a mere construct—it is the precondition of any statement about the world.

Harari wants to abolish the self—yet every sentence he writes is an expression of his thinking, his standpoint, his choice.

Without the self, there is no perspective.

Without perspective, no language.

Without language, no thought.

A world without self is not silent—it is speechless.

And without language, there can be no thought about the world.

2. Why Freedom Is Necessary to Recognize Truth

If everything is determined—if every thought
is merely the result of biochemistry—
then there is no longer any way to distinguish
between truth and error.

Because recognition requires distance:

the ability to confront a thought,

to examine it,

to reject or accept it—

on one's own initiative.

But if all "convictions" are just neural events,
then Harari's own conviction is nothing more
than a reaction.
He is not "convinced"—he is programmed.

And then this also applies to every reader.

It's not that he believes something because
it's true—he believes it because it happens in
him.

Freedom is the condition of the possibility of truth.
Without freedom—there is no knowledge, no insight, no progress.

3. Why Meaning Is the Prerequisite of Significance

If everything is meaningless—if every idea of purpose is an illusion—
then every act of communication is meaningless.

Because communication means:

I have something to say that matters to you.

But Harari says:

There is no meaning.
Everything is illusion.
Even what I am saying now.

So what remains?

Not truth.
Not wisdom.
Not orientation.

Only: noise.

A world without meaning is communicatively dead.

There are no questions—because there can be no answers.

There is no responsibility—because there is nothing to respond to.

There is no future—only processing without goal.

Conclusion: The Absolute Vacuum
What Harari proposes is not merely a new worldview—
it is a mode of thought that dissolves itself.

A world without self, freedom, and meaning cannot be thought—
it can only occur.
And even that—would be meaningless.

With this insight, our analysis comes to an end.

We have not refuted what Harari says—
we have shown that it cannot even be said.

Now the stage is set for the decisive question:

What is the human being—truly?

What Remains – and What Follows

In the first part of this book, we analyzed a worldview that has gained considerable influence in recent years.

Yuval Noah Harari represents a kind of thinking that presents itself with cool clarity, scientific language, and apparent neutrality—but in truth, it is something else:

A system of hollowing-out.

We have seen how this way of thinking dissolves the human being:

His self: denied.

His freedom: abolished.

His meaning: unmasked as illusion.

His value: reduced to data flow.

His future: rendered obsolete by artificial systems.

This worldview strips the human person to the core—elegantly, logically, but mercilessly.
It does not speak with the human being—it speaks about him, as if he were just one machine among many.

And yet:

The reader of this book knows that he exists, that he is alive.
He has not merely processed data—he has thought, felt, judged.
He was not neutral—he was involved.

And that is the point.

Because what remains, after we have followed Harari's worldview to its logical end, is not merely intellectual emptiness.
What remains is an inescapable sensation—an inner echo that cannot be silenced:

"I am—and I know that I am."

Another View Is Possible

Perhaps Harari is right about much of what he describes—
but perhaps he is wrong about what he excludes.

He sees data, patterns, behavior—but he does not see the one who sees.

He speaks of the brain—but he does not know consciousness.

He describes the world—but he recognizes no counterpart.

And yet every reader knows:

I think.

I choose.

I love.

I ask.

I suffer.

I seek.

And through it all remains a core that cannot be analyzed, dissected, or disenchanted.

A core that was not made—but given.
An innermost point that has never been fully wounded, never fully destroyed, never fully extinguished.

A silent, absolute center—

one that does not say: "I function,"
but: "I am."

The Turning Point: From Nothingness to Origin
What now follows from all of this?
What remains when Harari's vision reveals itself as empty—but the question still stands?

What follows is this:

The search for truth must begin with what is undeniable.
And the most undeniable thing a person knows is the fact of their own existence.

Not physical existence—but spiritual presence.
Consciousness. The self.

This experience—"I am"—is the point from
which all thinking begins.
And it is exactly there that we now begin.

For anyone who takes this point seriously will
come to see:

The "I am" is not relative—it is absolute.

It is not a product—it is origin.

It is not functional—it is essential.

And it points—inescapably—to a greater
origin,
one that is not energy, not a principle, not an
algorithm—
but a Self.

An absolute, eternal, spiritual Self.

The human being is not meaningless—he is
willed.

Not because an algorithm produced him,
but because a God called him.

Part II: The True Human – A Creature of God

Prologue to Part II: No Ideology Without Narratives

Part II begins – with an answer.
Not with an ideology.
Not with a counter-narrative.
But with a response to what the reader already knows – if they listen inwardly.

We ask:

Who am I?
Why do I exist?
Where does my consciousness come from?
Why is freedom real – and necessary?
What is meaning – and what does it mean that I seek it?

And we will show:

There is a truth about the human being.
A truth Harari could never see –
not because it is hidden in data,
but because it lives in the indestructible I.

Chapter 6 – The Indestructible "I": The Beginning of All Truth

1. The Immediate Experience of "I Am"

Before a human being reflects on themselves, before they name, describe, analyze, or understand themselves, something else happens—something much simpler, and yet far more profound:

They know that they are.

This knowledge is not learned.
It is not taught or mediated.
It is not the result of observation, argument, or cultural imprinting.
It is immediate.

Even before a child can say "I am," it lives in this awareness.
Even before reason awakens, there is this silent, unspoken certainty:

I exist.
I am here.
I am.

No one doubts their being
People may doubt everything:
God, the world, reality, the meaning of language, even their emotions.
But no one doubts that they exist.

Why?
Because doubt itself is only possible if there is someone who doubts.

Even Harari, who denies the self, can only say "There is no self" by speaking as a self.

No one asks, "Do I exist?"
The question "Do I exist?" is not only unanswerable—it is meaningless.
Because it already presupposes a consciousness that is asking.

Only the one who is can even ask whether they are.

The Self as Starting Point – Not as Conclusion
Throughout the history of philosophy, countless attempts have been made to define, relativize, or derive the self.

It has been described as a function, a linguistic game, a neurological illusion, or a psychological construct.

But all these theories come afterward.
They attempt to explain something that is already present—before explanation is even possible.

"I am" is not the conclusion of a theory.
It is its beginning.

Without this inner center, there is:

no consciousness,

no thought,

no ethics,

no relationship,

no understanding,

no responsibility.

Everything we know, experience, feel, or think begins at this one point:

I am.

A Consciousness Without Origin?
And here, the real search begins—which we now embark on together:

Where does this "I am" come from?

Why is it there—indestructible, unchanging, timeless, present?

Can something like this arise from matter?

Or is it the radiant sign of something else—of an origin that is not of this world?

These questions lead us to a radical point.
A point that is not speculative—but can be experienced by every person.

A point about which we can say with certainty:

It is the beginning of all truth.

2. Why Consciousness Cannot Be Reduced

Modern materialism claims:

Consciousness is an emergent property of highly complex neuronal processes.
In other words:
If you arrange enough matter in the right way, "subjective experience" somehow arises—
the sense of self, thought, and self-awareness.

But this belief—and it is indeed a belief—does not withstand serious scrutiny.

1. Emergence explains nothing
The word "emergence" sounds scientific—but often it is just a placeholder for what cannot be explained.
It says: We don't know how—but somehow it happens.

But how can material structure, which by definition is:

spatial,

temporal,

causally bound,

divisible and measurable,

bring forth something that is:

non-spatial,

non-temporal,

immeasurable,

indivisible,

not relative,

but absolutely present?

The "I"-consciousness is not composed of parts.
It is not "a little bit self" and "a little bit not-self."
It is whole, undivided, complete.

And precisely because of that, it cannot arise from matter.
Because matter knows no such indivisibility in the realm of spirit.

2. Self-awareness as a transmaterial phenomenon
Imagine observing your thoughts.
You watch your feelings.
You remember yourself.

Who is doing this?

Not your brain—you are.
Not your neurons—but your consciousness.

Consciousness is aware of itself.
It reflects. It knows itself. It recognizes itself.
And: it remains the same, even when everything else changes.

Your body ages.
Your opinions shift.
Your emotions fluctuate.

But the center of your perception—your "I am"—

remains identical.

This is not a metaphysical dogma—
it is an experience every human being knows.

And this experience is not localized.
It cannot be measured.
It cannot be extended.

Therefore, it cannot come from something
that has those properties.

3. The materialist fallacy
If consciousness truly arose from matter,
it would have to be explainable through
measurable state changes.

But:

You can observe neural processes—
yet you will not find a self within them.

You can establish correlations—
but not identity.

The self is not "in the brain."
It uses the brain—

but it is not contained in it.

The materialist fallacy lies in confusing
the interplay of brain regions with the reality
of consciousness.
But the brain is not the origin of the mind—
it is its instrument.

4. The consequence: A limit of natural science
Natural science can:

measure processes,

analyze structures,

quantify effects.

But it cannot answer:

Why there is something that recognizes itself.

Because this act of recognition is not derivable.
It is original.
It transcends matter.

The human being experiences themselves—
and this experience cannot be explained
by motion, weight, impulses, or electricity.

Conclusion:
Consciousness is:

not composable,

not manufacturable,

not simulatable,

not copyable.

It is an inner light
that can neither be produced by the brain
nor imitated by an algorithm.

And this light points—unmistakably—
to an origin beyond matter.

3. The Personal Self as an Ontological Fact

The human being does not merely know that he is.
He also knows that he is someone.

Not something.

Not a function.

Not a form.

But: a person.

This personal self is not a product of language, not a cultural construct, not a biological illusion.
It is what precedes all thinking, all feeling, all remembering, all deciding.

The I is the precondition—not the consequence.

You can study many aspects of a person:
Their abilities, their memories, their history.
You can analyze, compare, describe.

But behind all this stands something that cannot be explained, reduced, or reconstructed:

The fact that a person experiences themselves—
as an indivisible I.

This personal center is not composed of parts.
It is not a puzzle made of neural and psychological fragments.
It is a spiritual core of being—an origin point.

It is the one who experiences—not the experienced.
It is the one who thinks—not the thought.
It is the one who chooses—not the option.
It is the inner point of unity from which all subjective life arises.

You can be mistaken about many things: your memories, your perceptions, your judgments.
But you cannot be mistaken about the fact that you are someone.

Even doubt itself presupposes that someone is doubting.

This personhood is not a psychological accident.
It is not a product of evolutionary fashion.
Nor is it a mere effect of social interaction.

It is what makes the human being what they are:
A spiritual being that knows itself—
and knows that it is not arbitrary.

The person is not an appearance, but a reality.
A reality that cannot be explained—
but must be acknowledged.

It is not a passing self-image—
but an ontological fact.
Something that is,
and that cannot be destroyed by analysis, technology, or deconstruction.

Even if all knowledge, all memory, all language were to vanish—

the I that looks into the world and experiences it as world would remain.

That is why we say:

The human being is not a whim of evolution,
but a being intended.
Willed.
Called.

And this personal nature is the first sign of their origin—
not in matter,
but in a Personhood that exists before the world.

In the next chapter, we will follow this sign further—
and ask what it means that the human is not only someone who is,
but someone who is free.

Chapter 7 – Freedom: The Prerequisite of All Responsibility

1. What Freedom Truly Means

If one follows Harari's line of thought, it quickly becomes clear:
The concept of free will has no place in his worldview.
What humans perceive as freedom of choice is—within his model—nothing more than the result of biochemical processes, stimulus-response patterns, and unconscious conditioning.
In this framework, freedom is not a reality, but an illusion.

And yet, it is exactly that—a reality.
A reality that every human being experiences daily:
In decisions.
In doubts.
In guilt.
In love.

But what exactly is this freedom?

First of all, it is not what many people today think it is.

Freedom is not arbitrariness. It is not impulsiveness. It is not simply the absence of restrictions.

Whoever thinks that being free means doing whatever one wants, whenever and with whomever, confuses freedom with instinct.

Such a notion misses the essential core of true freedom.

True freedom is the capacity for conscious, responsible choice—
not in a vacuum, but in the light of truth.

A person is truly free not merely when choosing between options,
but when they recognize what is good and choose it,
even if it comes at a cost.

Freedom is not revealed in the escape from boundaries—
but in inner maturity,
in a choice aligned with truth.

The freedom given to the human being is not a static condition.

It is a capacity—
a potential that actualizes in every conscious
decision.
It is not an automatic function of the brain,
but an act of the spirit.
It is not an illusion—
but the very place where human dignity re-
sides.

Because only one who is free can be responsible.
Only one who can choose can act morally or
immorally.
Only one who can say no can ever truly say
yes.

A helpful distinction is found in the classical
differentiation between "freedom from" and
"freedom to":

"Freedom from" refers to the absence of external coercion—
violence, pressure, fear, or control.
This kind of freedom is important—
but it is not enough.

Only "freedom to"—the inner ability to recognize and choose the good—
is the real freedom that matters.

A person may be outwardly unbound and yet inwardly enslaved.
Conversely, someone may sit in prison—
and still be inwardly free,
because they refuse to bow to evil.

External conditions say little about a person's freedom.
What matters is:
Do they act from insight?
From truth?
From love?

This dimension of freedom is not material.
It is not derivable.
It cannot be manufactured.

Like the "I", it points to a spiritual reality.
To an origin that is not deterministic—
but free in itself.

In the next section, we will explore this further:

Why human freedom can only be explained
if there is a free, personal origin—
a God who is Himself an "I",
and who not only permits freedom—
but wills it.

2. The Capacity to Choose as a Reflection of Divine Freedom

Human freedom is not merely a functional instrument.
It is not a practical by-product of the brain, accidentally fitting into the logic of evolution.
Nor is it the result of social conditioning or cultural imprinting.
It is—in its truest sense—a form of likeness to the Creator.

Man is free because the God who created him is free.
He can choose because he comes from a Being that creates not out of compulsion, but by sovereign will.

This opens up a perspective fundamentally inconceivable within materialist systems:
Freedom is not a quirk of nature—
but a gift of grace.
An expression of the fact that man was not merely made—
but called.
He was not programmed—
but addressed.

Only one who is addressed can respond.
Only one who can respond is truly free.

This capacity to choose is not a sign of weakness,
but the highest expression of what sets man apart from the animal—
and what unites him with the Divine.

Animals act by instinct, drive, or programming.
Humans, on the other hand, can act against their impulses, against their fears, against their self-interest—
from inner conviction.

That conviction does not arise from matter, from chance, or from utility—
but from the spirit that recognizes truth and turns toward it.

If a person is capable of choosing between good and evil,
between truth and falsehood,
between self-giving and selfishness,
they do not do so because a biological system compels them—

but because within them lives an inner capacity that transcends biology:

The will.

This will is not irrational.
On the contrary:
It is the highest form of spiritual activity.
It is the place where reason and love,
knowledge and decision, meet.

In every free decision a human being makes,
he either fulfills himself—or he misses himself.
He becomes more of what he is meant to
be—
or he turns away from it.
He answers the call—
or he refuses it.

This capacity to choose can only be explained
if its origin lies not below,
but above the human being.

Only a free God can create free creatures.
Only an "I" that is sovereign can call forth another "I" that is allowed to respond—

not forced to.

That is why free will points to something higher.
It is not the final mystery of biology—
but the Creator's seal upon His creation.

Because God did not want robots.
Not automatons.
Not flawless yet unfree replicas.

He wanted counterparts.

Beings who can respond.

Beings who can love—because they are free.

Beings who can recognize Him—because they are not mere reflections, but persons.

Human freedom, then, is not merely an ethical tool—
it is a metaphysical sign.

It says:
Man is willed as a being who is free—
to be loved and to love.

In the next section, we will explore what follows from this freedom:
for ethics, for responsibility, for conscience—
and for love itself.

3. Responsibility, Love, Conscience – Meaningless Without Freedom

If man were not free, there would be no guilt—
but also no responsibility.
There would be no moral greatness—
but also no dignity.
There would be no failure—
but also no true triumph.

For where the will is not free, man is no more than an animal,
reacting to inner or outer stimuli.

And so, every form of ethics begins with a silent, yet inescapable assumption:

Man can choose—
and he is responsible for what he chooses.

Responsibility is not a feeling.
It is not merely a function of social behavior or upbringing.
It is the ability of a free being to respond to a standard that stands above him.

He who cannot act otherwise bears no responsibility.
But he who could have acted differently—and did not—stands in debt.

In every internal judgment we make about our own behavior, this truth is already present:

I could have acted differently.

I could have been honest.

I could have been faithful.

I could have resisted.

But if free will does not exist,
then every form of guilt is an illusion.
Then even the conscience—this quiet, uncomfortable witness within us—
is merely a disturbance in neuronal harmony.
Then the call to goodness is nothing more than conditioning.
Then ethics becomes system maintenance,
and morality mere socio-technical management.

And yet, deep down, we know: this is not true.
We know that we make choices—
and that every choice leaves a mark, not only in the world,
but in ourselves.

Perhaps the most powerful expression of this truth is love.

Love is not instinct.
Not need.
Not mechanism.
Love is the freest of all emotions,
and at the same time the most conscious of all acts of will.

No one can be forced to love.
No one can be obligated to open themselves, to give themselves,
to make themselves vulnerable, to remain faithful.

Love is either free—or it is not love at all.

And that is why love is only possible because man is free.

Without freedom, there is no love—
only adaptation, possession, control, or self-
erasure.
Without freedom, there is no ethics—
only moralism, pressure, or calculation.
Without freedom, there is no conscience—
only fear, guilt reflexes, or conformity.

That is why freedom is the foundation of all
that is higher in the human being:

of responsibility,

of remorse,

of repentance,

of compassion,

of self-giving,

of truthfulness,

of love.

In a world without freedom, there would be
no guilt—

but also no forgiveness.
No failure—
but also no grace.
No loss—
but also no true closeness.

He who denies man his freedom denies him his humanity.
For without freedom, only what Harari describes remains:
control, conditioning, optimization—
but no inner life, no you, no I, no truth, no mercy.

That is why it is no coincidence that Harari's worldview feels so cold, so empty, so mechanical in the end.

Where there is no freedom, there can be no warmth.
And where there is no warmth, there is no human being.

In the next chapter, we ask a new question— one that shines through everything:

What is the meaning of life—and can it really be just an illusion?

Chapter 8 – The Meaning of Life

1. Why Meaning Is Not a Projection

One of the most astonishing and profound traits of the human being is their capacity to ask about meaning.

Not just occasionally, not only in special circumstances, but as a fundamental movement of existence itself.

Even if they cannot put it into words, a person still lives out of this question—often hidden, sometimes desperate, occasionally repressed, but never entirely extinguished.

"What's the point of it all?"
"What is the reason?"
"Why am I alive?"
"Is there something that endures, that holds, that matters?"

These questions are not cultural oddities. They are not taught. They do not arise from religious upbringing or philosophical reading.

They arise from within the human being, from the very core of their nature—

from the fact that they do not merely live, but know they live, and ask why.

Modern theory has tried to interpret this search for meaning as a projection.
It claims that meaning is not something to be discovered, but something invented—a psychological aid to help cope with the uncertainty of existence. A kind of internal myth humans construct to make their biological lives bearable.

But this theory is not only cynical—it is unsustainable.

Because if meaning were just a construct, the question of meaning would be arbitrary.
There would be no objective urgency, no depth, no awe, no being-gripped.
But that is exactly what does happen:

Human beings are moved by the question of meaning.
It does not let them go.
It is not neutral—it is existential.

And that shows:

Meaning is not merely a product. It is an echo.
An echo of something that does not originate in us, but speaks within us.

Meaning can be experienced—and that alone is enough to say:

It is not simply subjective.
Because no one would risk, build, or sacrifice an entire life for something they themselves had invented.
Those who follow an inner calling, who act in love, who sacrifice, who hold on to the truth even at great cost—
they do not act that way because it is psycho-logically helpful.
They act that way because they know it is right.
Because they have sensed something greater than themselves.

Meaning cannot be manufactured. It can only be discovered.
Just as beauty cannot be created, only seen.
Just as love cannot be planned, only given.
Just as truth cannot be invented, only found.

And there is more:
The very fact that human beings ask is already the first clue to an answer.

Because no one sincerely asks about something they are certain does not exist.
The question itself is a trace—a sign that something is meant.

Human beings ask about meaning because something answers within them before they find the words.
They know that there is more.
Not because they were told—
but because something within them speaks:
a silent knowledge that does not argue, but calls.

In the next section, we will follow that call—
and ask what it means when a person feels called.
Because at that point, meaning is no longer merely an echo—it becomes a conversation.

2. Purpose, Calling, Transcendence – The Voice That Means Us

The question of meaning is more than an inner impulse, more than intellectual curiosity or emotional longing.
It is an existential sign pointing to something greater than ourselves—
and yet, it is something that speaks to us.

Because the one who asks is not just searching in general.
He asks for himself.
He wants to know what his life means, what purpose it serves, what place he occupies in this vast, often incomprehensible whole.

And it is here that something incomprehensible occurs:

The question of meaning does not point back to ourselves—
but to something else.
Or more precisely: to someone.

Because the human being does not just experience himself as questioning—

but often, as being called.

Not by a voice.
Not by words.
But through an inner sense that runs deeper than thoughts:

There is a purpose.

There is a direction.

There is something that awaits me.

This experience is difficult to name, but familiar to many.
Sometimes it happens in moments of silence.
Sometimes in the face of death.
Sometimes at the birth of a child.
Or in those rare moments when you suddenly know: This is my path.

This experience is not a construct.
It cannot be planned, manufactured, or repeated.
It is relationship—not system, not technique.

The human being experiences himself as addressed—
and this being-addressed is not an illusion.
It is not the product of desire or imagination.
In fact, it often contradicts both.

The call does not come because we desire it.
It comes because we are meant.

In this experience of calling, something is revealed:
That the human being does not belong to himself.
That his life is not a closed circuit.
That his existence does not merely reflect back upon itself,
but is from the beginning open—toward something beyond him.

Those who feel called know:
I am not here merely to function.
I am not just one organism among many.
I am willed.

And this being-willed is the opposite of arbitrariness.
It gives life direction, depth, and meaning—

because it comes from a source not within us,
but from what we call transcendence—
and what is more than a word.
It is the reality in which we are rooted, without having invented it.

If calling is real, then the meaning of life is not something we assign to it—
but something that has been given to us.

Meaning is not a psychological framework.
Meaning is a form of relationship:
Between the one who speaks—
and the one who hears.

That is why every serious question of meaning will, sooner or later, lead to the question:

Who is speaking?
Who means me?

In the next section, we will ask this question openly - and follow the clue that only a person can give meaning.
And that relationship with God is not an idea
- but a spiritual reality.

3. Personal Relationship with a Personal Origin

We have seen that meaning does not simply arise because we need it.
It is not the result of intellectual effort or emotional longing.
It meets us—like a voice, a call, an inner knowing.
And with that, one thing becomes unmistakably clear:

Meaning can only come from a counterpart.
From something—or better: someone—greater than we are, and yet capable of addressing us.

Meaning is not neutral.
It is not like a law of nature that operates whether or not someone is there to receive it.
It is always directed—toward me. Toward you. Toward a singular I.

And therefore, only a person can give meaning.

Not a principle. Not an abstract world spirit.
Not an idea, not a force, not an evolutionary
mechanism.

But rather: a personal origin—an I that calls
to us because it knows us.
A God who is not function, but subject.
A God who is not something, but someone.

When a human being experiences himself as
a person who is questioned, called, loved,
judged, remembered, addressed—
then the most natural, most powerful, most
coherent conclusion is this:

He stands in relationship to another I.
To a God who is not principle, but presence.
Not an abstraction, but a face.

This relationship is not a worldview.
It is not a theory.
It is not a religious construction.

It is—for the one who has once sensed it at
its core—a spiritual reality.

A reality that does not come from the outside,
but speaks from within—with a clarity that does not rest on argument,
but on the unmistakable experience of being meant.

It is remarkable how many people resist the thought of God as person.
As energy, as force, as "something," He may still be acceptable—
but as You, as a living reality with will, love, and patience?

And yet:
Only a You can call to us.
Only an I can mean us.
Only a person can say: "I have called you by your name; you are mine."

This is not metaphor.
It is the deepest reality a human being can encounter.

Whoever begins to recognize this relationship—not as an idea, but as experience—
his life changes.

Not because a concept shifts,
but because he is suddenly no longer alone.

He stands in the light of Another.
He no longer speaks into the void.
His "I am" meets the divine "I AM"—
and in this encounter, theory does not arise,
but truth.

This truth is not abstract. It is existential.
It transforms not only thought, but being.

That is why we say:

Man does not find his meaning within himself—
but in the You who created him.
In the personal origin who says of himself:
"I AM WHO I AM."

In the next chapter, we will ask: Who is this origin—
and why can He not be impersonal, anonymous, or abstract?

Chapter 9 – The Origin: Why God Must Be an "I"

1. Why Only a Personal God Can Create the "I"

We have seen that man is an I—
a personal, indivisible, inwardly experienced center of consciousness.
This I is not the product of external circumstances,
not a composite algorithm,
not a biological artifact.
It is the innermost core of being human—irreducible, inexplicable, inimitable.

And this raises the question:

Where does it come from?
What is the origin of the I?
And can that origin be anything other than—
once again—an I?

Many philosophical and spiritual systems have attempted to imagine this origin as impersonal.

They speak of a source, an energy, a ground
of being, a law, a field.
But all these models leave a gap:

No principle can give rise to a subject.
No impersonal something can give birth to a
personal I.
No function creates freedom.
And no abstract whole produces an individ-
ual You.

Individuality is not an accident.
Nor is it a fragment broken off from some
collective primal consciousness.
Because if the I were merely a wave in the
ocean of being,
then its personality would be an illusion—
and with it, all responsibility, all love, all conscience, all meaning.

But we have shown:

The I is real.

It is absolute.

It is experiential—and it knows itself.

Therefore, its origin must likewise be personal.
Because:

Only an I can will another I into being.

Only a will can generate individuality.

Only a person can encounter another person.

A collective—of any kind—cannot create true individuality.
Because the many can only form parts, never a unified whole in itself.
Yet the I is not merely a function within a greater system.
It is not an interchangeable module, not a placeholder, not an emergent phenomenon.

It is an unmistakable entity that cannot be substituted.
A child may resemble the father—but he is not the father.
A student may learn from the teacher—but he remains himself.

This uniqueness of the I can only be explained if it was intended—
not by something, but by someone.
By an origin that does not generalize, but wills distinction.

Thus, the only sustainable origin of the I is:

A personal God.

A God who is not principle, but person.

A God who says, "I AM WHO I AM."

A God who creates other Is because He desires relationship—not just structure.

A God who loves—and therefore calls persons who are capable of love.

Only such a God can be the Father of the I.
Everything else remains projection, construction—or void.

In the next section, we will ask why spirit cannot arise from matter—

and why life can only come from life, and consciousness only from consciousness.

2. The Impossibility of Mind Arising from Dead Matter

Anyone who examines today's common explanatory models for consciousness, thought, will, or the structure of the self quickly encounters a seemingly coherent narrative:

Mind, it is said, is a product of neural complexity.

If matter is sufficiently organized, networked, and stimulated, then—so the assumption goes—consciousness will eventually emerge.

This idea has seeped so deeply into our cultural understanding that it is rarely questioned anymore.

And yet:

It is not only unproven—it is logically impossible.

For mind and matter differ not merely in degree, but in essence.

Matter is:

spatial,

extended,

divisible,

measurable,

causally bound,

passive.

Mind is:

non-spatial,

unextended,

immeasurable,

indivisible,

not explainable by causality,

active, self-referential, and intentional.

So whoever claims that mind can "arise from" matter must explain how properties entirely alien to mind could suddenly produce a conscious being.

But that is—under sober consideration—a contradiction.

One especially compelling image expresses this truth clearly:

Life comes from life—consciousness from consciousness.

Just as there is not a single piece of evidence that life has ever arisen from dead matter, there is likewise no evidence that an I, a self-awareness, or a free will has ever emerged from inanimate material.

The knowledge "I am" cannot be constructed.
It cannot be simulated.
It cannot be programmed.
It can only arise through a reality that is itself an I—and capable of calling, willing, and creating another I.

The attempt to reduce spirit to matter ultimately leads to a grotesque inversion of reality:

The higher is said to come from the lower.

The active from the reactive.

Freedom from determination.

Meaning from meaninglessness.

Thought from motion.

Consciousness from chance.

But every experience, every act of reflection, every thought about one's own thinking reveals:

There is no bridge from dead matter to the living self.
The origin of spirit must itself be spiritual—
otherwise it remains incomprehensible.

Therefore we say:

Just as there can be no father who was never a son,
so there can be no spirit that does not come from spirit.

God is not the result of a process—
He is the source of mind—
and that alone is why man is capable of spirit.

In the next section, we will explore what follows from this:
If man is not the product of chance but is willed as a person,
then he bears within him an eternal seal—
a calling that reaches beyond this life.

3. The Response to the Call: Man as an Eternally Intended Person

When we look back at what we've said about the self—its indivisibility, its freedom, its capacity to love, its search for meaning—it becomes undeniably clear:

This I is not a biological fluke.
Not an evolutionary intermediate.
Not a temporary phenomenon on the way to something higher.

No—this I is willed.
Not as a mass, not as a function, not as a variable in a system.
But as a person.

And not merely as one person among many—
but as a unique, unrepeatable, spiritual being that can never be duplicated.

The I is not copyable—because it arose from the depth of an infinite intention.

The biblical term for this is "image."

Man is created in the image of God—not in outer form, but in innermost essence.

He is not God, but he carries something divine within him.

He is not omnipotent, but he is free.

He is not omniscient, but he recognizes truth.

He is not omnipresent, but he is capable of love.

An algorithm can calculate, learn, even combine creatively.

But it cannot forgive.

It cannot sacrifice.

It cannot take responsibility.

And it cannot love.

Only a being that knows it is—and that it is meant—can do such things.

This calling to personhood, to freedom, to relationship—
it does not end with death.
It is not limited to the body, to the years, to
memory.

Because the I is not bound by space and
time.
It is not biologically formed, not neuron-
bound, not materially localized.
It is a spiritual core that does not age, does
not decay, does not perish.

Therefore, the idea that the I ceases to exist
at death is not just sad—
it is incoherent.

How can something indivisible disintegrate?
How can that which is experienced outside
space and time be ended by an event within
space and time?
How can what was eternally called suddenly
fall silent?

The immortality of man is not wishful thinking.
It is the natural consequence of his structure.

Whoever is an I—is so forever.

And that means:
Man is not on the path to dissolution,
but on the path to an encounter with the
One who called him.

His life is not a cycle, not a repetition, not a
fleeting passage.
It is a journey—and that journey has a goal.

In the next chapter, we will ask what follows
from this realization for life here and now:
What does it mean to live in a world with
God?
What hope, what dignity, what future does
that open up?

Chapter 10 – A World with God: Hope, Dignity, Future

1. What Remains of Man—When God Is Gone

When God is removed from the world, it is not just a metaphysical concept that disappears.
It is not merely a religious idea or an outdated worldview that vanishes.

What disappears is the center of order.
The inner cohesion of human existence breaks apart.

Because God is not a hypothesis that can be believed or dismissed like a theory.
If He exists, He is the ground of all grounds, the source of all meaning, the measure of all things.
If this origin is denied, everything loses its place, its depth, its foundation.

So what remains of man when this origin is missing?

First: Nihilism.

Without God, there is no ultimate purpose, no final value, no highest good.
What remains is an eternal "Why not?"

Why not live for pleasure?

Why not die of boredom?

Why not destroy what disturbs me?

Without God, man becomes the measure of himself—
and thereby also the final judge of good and evil, life and death, truth and falsehood.
But a standard that sets itself is no longer a standard at all.

Second: Isolation.

Without God, the deepest point of reference is missing.
Relationship becomes purely horizontal— person to person, I to you.

But if this I is no longer anchored, if it is merely function, fleeting identity, a neural construct—
then the you also becomes uncertain, intangible, blurry.
There is no final binding force anymore, no fidelity, no enduring ground.
Relationships become temporary alliances, love becomes negotiation,
responsibility becomes an option.

Third: Fragmentation.

When man no longer knows where he comes from, why he exists, where he is heading—
he becomes internally torn apart.
He lives in the present, without origin or destination.
He jumps from desire to desire, from idea to idea, from identity to identity.
He reinvents himself—again and again—because there is no inner core that sustains him.
Everything becomes fluid. Everything becomes possible. Everything becomes arbitrary.
And in this arbitrariness, man loses himself.

And finally: Death.

If there is no God, then death is the absolute end.
No continuation. No meaning. No judgment.
No comfort. No homecoming.

Man dies—
and disappears.
Not just his body,
but also his thoughts, his decisions, his love,
his pain.
Everything fades—
as if it had never existed.

This is the price of a world without God:

Man becomes finite, fragmented, arbitrary—
and in the end: annihilated.

In the next section, we will show what changes
when man realizes that he has been called—
and that God is not absent, but waiting.

2. What Man Can Become—When God Is Recognized

If God exists—and is recognized—then not only does man's worldview change.
His self-image, his experience of life, and his inner attitude toward the world are transformed as well.

Because the recognition of God is not an intellectual conclusion.
It is an encounter that orders, uplifts, and transforms a person in their deepest core.

Identity
The person who recognizes God suddenly knows who he is.
Not because someone has assigned him a new role,
but because he sees his origin—and with it, hears his inner name.

He is no longer just someone who has become,
but someone who was willed into being.

He is no longer merely the result of genetics, socialization, and coincidence—
but a being conceived, intended, and called.

This realization gives a depth of identity that nothing external can ever bestow.
It carries even when everything else falls away—success, recognition, achievement, even health.
Because man is no longer "someone because..."—
but:

Someone—because God sees him.

Responsibility
The recognition of God does not mean relief—but elevation.
It does not free one from responsibility—it grounds it.
For only one who sees himself as a free, willed I
can also understand himself as someone

who can and should respond.

Responsibility then becomes not a burden,
but an honor.
Not a threat, but a mark of dignity.

It makes man a co-creator,
a witness,
a bearer of light in a dark world.

He no longer lives only for himself.
He knows:

My life carries weight—because it must answer a call.

Spiritual Maturity
The recognition of God leads to an inner transformation
that can be described by the word maturity.
It does not make a person perfect—but truthful.
Not faultless—but ready to take responsibility.
Not all-knowing—but capable of humility.

The person who recognizes God begins to see life within a larger horizon.
He is not crushed by the greatness of God—

but carried by it.
He is not diminished—
but lifted up, because he knows what he is
living for.

Hope and Purpose
Perhaps the most decisive difference between a world with God and one without
God is this:

In the world with God, there is a goal.
And this goal is not invented—but promised.

It was given to us, not because we deserved it,
but because we were called to reach it.

Hope is then not optimism,
not a psychological strategy against fear,
but a knowledge—
carried by a promise that does not come
from us, but was given for us.

The person who recognizes God
does not begin a new life—
he begins his true life.

He does not become religious—he becomes real.

He is not externally controlled—he is led home.

In the next—and final—section of this chapter, we will show
that this path is not a construction,
but a return to the origin.

A homecoming—into the light that never fades.

3. Outlook: A New Path – Not a Construction, but a Homecoming

We live in a time where almost everything is
being reconstructed:
identity, truth, morality—even reality itself.
It seems as if man can design himself—
and that this very act is the mark of his maturity.

But what if the opposite is true?
What if true maturity lies not in reinventing
oneself,
but in rediscovering oneself?

What if the "new path" so many seek
is, in truth, a return—
back to what has always been there,
what has carried us long before we could
name it?

Not progress—but homecoming.
Not a construct—but the rediscovery of
origin.

For in all human searching—
in philosophy, science, spirituality, art—

a quiet undertone resonates:

I am not at home.
Something is missing.
I am on a journey—but where to?

This restlessness is not a flaw.
It is a sign.
It does not point us to a new system,
but to a relationship
that has never been broken,
only buried.

The return to God is not a regression into old
structures.
It is not an escape from modernity,
nor a surrender to complexity.

It is the answer to a call
that has never stopped speaking.

Whoever hears this call—not as a voice, but
as an inner knowing—
stands at a crossroads:

Do I wish to keep constructing, optimizing,
controlling?

Or do I wish to listen, receive, respond?

This decision is not external.
It takes place deep within—
where the I knows it is meant.

Because God does not force.
He calls.
He does not push.
He waits.

But His waiting is not silence.
It is an invitation—
to truth.
To clarity.
To turning back.
To freedom.

The new path we speak of is therefore not a
suggestion.
It is a possibility that responds to truth.

It does not lead to an ideal,
but to a You.

To the You who has always been there,
and who, in the beginning, said:

"I am."

And who now—at the end of all human con-
structions—
calls out to us again:

"I am here. Come home."

Final Word: The Choice Between Coldness and Light

At the end of all analysis, comparisons, and arguments, something remains
that cannot be weighed, delegated, or relativized:

The decision.

A person can leave many questions unanswered—
about politics, science, ideologies, and concepts.
But the question of oneself cannot be postponed forever.
For it is always present—
and it becomes more urgent as everything else falls apart.

There is no neutrality.
Those who think they can stay out of it
are choosing silence.
But silence, too, is an answer.

Today—more than ever—

humanity stands between two radically op-
posing worldviews:

On one side:

Dissolution.
The end of the self.
The denial of freedom.
The disenchantment of meaning.
The coldness of mechanism.
Death as the final truth.

And on the other:

Truth.
The indestructible self.
Freedom as a gift.
Meaning as encounter.
Love as the answer.
God—as origin, destiny, and counterpart.

This contrast can be named in many ways.
But perhaps the clearest formulation is this:

Between robot—and living being.
Between the human as data point—and the
human as image-bearer.

Between control—and trust.
Between construction—and calling.
Between emptiness—and fullness.
Between coldness—and light.

This choice is not merely intellectual.
It is existential.
Because whoever chooses dissolution,
chooses against themselves—
against their heart, their conscience, their innermost knowing.

But whoever listens
to the voice that has spoken within them
since the beginning
will discover:

They are not alone.
They never were.
They are not lost.
They are called.

And this call is not general.
It is personal.
It is for you.
Now.

The decision is real—
and it begins in the innermost being.

Where all else becomes silent.
Where no concept remains.
Where only one thing is left:

"I am—and I answer."

Appendix

This appendix summarizes the line of argument presented in Part II in a condensed form.

The "I am" Consciousness and Its Metaphysical Implications

1. The "I am" Consciousness as a Starting Point

Every human being knows immediately and without doubt: "I am."
This awareness of one's own existence is universal—shared by all eight billion people. It is absolute, unchanging, and requires no external confirmation.
The question "Am I?" is absurd, because it can only be asked by someone who already exists.
This "I am" consciousness is the undeniable starting point of our reflections— a self-evident fact that needs no further justification.

2. The Absoluteness of Consciousness

The "I am" consciousness is unchanging—it remains the same regardless of time, place, condition, or external circumstance.

If consciousness were a product of material processes (e.g., neural activity in the brain), it would be subject to change, since all matter is perishable and mutable.

But that is not the case: the "I am" consciousness is absolute and therefore cannot have a material origin.

It must have a metaphysical, transcendent source beyond the physical world.

Possible Objections

A. Neural Changes:
Changes in brain activity—such as in sleep or coma—affect only thoughts or perceptions, not the core of "I am," which remains intact.

B. The Illusion Thesis:
A possible objection is that the "I am" consciousness is an illusion produced by complex neurological processes.
This idea, espoused by neuroscientists like Daniel Dennett and in some philosophical or

religious systems (e.g., Buddhism, Advaita Vedanta), fails due to circular reasoning:
To claim that consciousness is an illusion, one already requires consciousness to perceive the illusion.
Without consciousness, there is no one to experience an illusion.
Thus, the illusion thesis presupposes exactly what it attempts to explain—and is therefore logically self-contradictory.

3. The Personal, Transcendent Source

Since the "I am" consciousness is absolute, its source must also be conscious, volitional, and individual.
Only a personal being—a God with consciousness, will, and attributes—can create consciousness, life, and free will.
A diffuse or impersonal origin (e.g., a homogeneous energy within transcendence) would lack both the intention and the capacity to bring forth individual consciousness.
Consciousness gives rise to consciousness, and life gives rise to life.
Thus, a person is required—and this personal God is the transcendent source of all being.

Possible Objections:

A. Panpsychism:
Approaches like panpsychism, which view consciousness as a universal property of matter, fail to explain how individual "I am" consciousnesses arise and often tend toward a collective consciousness that denies individuality.

B. Emanation or Collective Consciousness:
Some philosophies—like aspects of Eastern religions or Western New Age concepts— suggest that consciousness emanates from an impersonal source or is part of a collective consciousness.
This approach is rejected here because individuality is a central principle of the "I am."
Life and consciousness are always individually organized—both in the body and in the mind.
There is no such thing as collective consciousness.
Such a model would bypass personal responsibility and relationship with a personal God, and is often seen as a way to evade moral accountability toward the Creator.

4. Free Will and Life

The "I am" consciousness is inseparable from free will and life.
Free will is an inherent property of the "I am."
It arises directly from consciousness and enables human beings to make decisions.
Whereas God's will is absolutely free (God can create universes by an act of will and override natural laws through miracles), human will is relative—limited by the physical world and natural laws.
Yet human will can overcome secondary influences such as psychological or social pressures.

Life itself is the material expression of consciousness, but it is not purely material.
It arises when consciousness turns toward matter—and ends when this connection is severed (physical death).
Since consciousness is transcendent, it survives death and remains eternal.
The "I am" core is an indivisible unity and thus eternally existent.

5. Love and Perfect Beatitude

Free will enables the human being to choose for or against their Creator, God.

This choice is the foundation of authentic relationship, for only free will allows true love or rejection—manifested in closeness to or separation from God.

The love of God and the turning toward Him is the highest fulfillment of human existence. Only through free decision is an authentic relationship with God possible—one of friendship and love.

This perfect beatitude—proximity to God—is fully realized only in the transcendent realm, after the death of the physical body.

The "I am" consciousness remains eternally individual, for individuality is a core feature of consciousness.

Conclusion

From the indisputable "I am" consciousness, a coherent worldview is gradually derived: Consciousness is absolute and transcendent; it originates in a personal God; it is inseparable from free will and life; and it finds its fulfillment in a personal, loving relationship with God.

Objections such as emergence, illusion, or collective consciousness fail due to logical inconsistencies or denial of personal responsibility.

This line of reasoning offers a clear, logical, and profound explanation of the nature of consciousness and its significance for human life.

Other English-Language Books by the Same Author

Proof of the Existence of God:
Why a Conscious Creator Is the Only Explanation.

BoD Verlag, 2024
ISBN 9783759796851

A Conscious Choice for Faith
The Deliberate Return to God as Salvation from Crisis

BoD Verlag, 2024
ISBN 9783759794949

The Veneration of the Blessed Virgin Mary
A guide to understanding the Mother of God for reformed Christians and people of other faiths.

BoD Verlag, 2023
ISBN 9783757830595

All publications are available as paperback and e-book editions.